T0146979

EXPRESS WITH
LESS

A Mini Memoir by
An Aspiring Minimalist

Nancy Hoffman

authorHOUSE®

AuthorHouse™
1663 Liberty Drive
Bloomington, IN 47403
www.authorhouse.com
Phone: 1 (800) 839-8640

Published by AuthorHouse 12/13/2019

ISBN: 978-1-7283-2883-6 (sc)
ISBN: 978-1-7283-2882-9 (e)

Print information available on the last page.

This book is printed on acid-free paper.

CONTENTS

I dedicate this book to my stellar husband Roger. He is my rock and the love of my life. He is my biggest cheerleader and best example of a minimalist that I know. NH

PROLOGUE

The other day I was driving by the church around the corner, and an electronic billboard caught my eye. The kind of sign that with the touch of a finger will change messages and make beautiful graphics. A somewhat expensive looking sign. State of the art so to speak.

That sign took me back many, many years, to a time in the early 1960s when I was in Junior High school. I was very involved with the youth group at Childs Park Methodist Church. We were a close-knit group of about twenty kids, who not only went to church together, many of us attended the same school. And most of us grew up together. Our parents, for the most part, attended Childs Park Church, and were all friends. It was an extended family.

A new, young minister, Jim Dale, around age thirty, Rev. Jim Dale, arrived one day when I was in Junior High. I first met him on the steps that led to the fellowship hall. I walked over to the church from my house, a stone's throw away. I asked if Rev. Dale would like to join the Junior High Methodist Youth Fellowship Group, or M.Y.F., for pizza. He obliged and became an inspiration to the youth of our church. Being younger,

REV. JIM DALE

he could relate to our age group. He listened to us, joked with us and was there for us. A big fan of the Beatles and Simon and Garfunkel, (both popular singing groups of the day), Rev. Dale sometimes played one of their songs at the start of his sermon. He had an exceptional talent of weaving the meaning of the words in the song, to his topic of the day. It's easy to understand how well the youth bonded with him.

I chuckle sometimes and wonder if the "older generation" might have thought it irreverent to broadcast those secular songs over the speakers during Sunday church service, but to my knowledge no one complained. And the songs, like "Fool on the Hill" by the Beatles and "The Sound of Silence" by Simon and Garfunkel certainly resonated with the youth.

Our M.Y.F. met on Wednesday nights and Sunday mornings and evenings. The whole group was in the choir, and even though I am probably tone-deaf, I still held a spot in the choir loft. Singing in the choir, I felt like I was contributing to the church in some way. And I was part of the group. Everyone was welcome, whether you were pitch-perfect, or not. Thank goodness for that.

But one job I particularly liked, besides singing in the choir, was changing the sermon title every week on the simple, non-electronic sign that stood on the north side of the church property. It was a simple metal sign with a glass door.

Our house was only a block away from the church, so it was easy for me to walk over anytime I wanted. Sometime each

CHILDS PARK CHURCH

Monday, I would gather the box of white plastic letters from the church office, along with the title of the sermon, and head outside to change the prior week's sermon to the current week. I would unlock the glass door, take off the letters from the previous week, file those letters back, then hang the current letters in their proper slots. A simple thing. But, now, more than fifty years later, I remember it like yesterday. It gave me a good feeling. A sense of accomplishment. It was a responsibility that I didn't take lightly and one small thing that was building my character.

Thinking about this fancy sign I saw the other day, in front of that church around the corner, I wondered who changes the message? Who is that person who types the sermon title into the computer? Does it mean to them, what it did to me? Most likely not. I am relatively sure it is someone who works in the church office and quickly does it on their way to their lunch break. And they don't give it a second thought. I am not criticizing. I know it's just a "sign" of the times.

Times have changed. I get that. I do try to change with the times. Somewhat. We have to. We must. I don't think I want to go back to wringer washers and clotheslines.

But there is a little place in my heart where I long for the time when a young girl would gather up all those plastic letters, the paper with the sermon title written on it, the key to un-lock the sign, and go outside in the sunshine, to do a small job that meant something big to her. That is a nostalgic moment for me. I am left wondering what the nostalgic moments will be for the current generation?

When I think of minimalism, I think in terms of living a simpler life. A life that is perhaps reminiscent of the fifties and sixties. And, yes, unfortunately, there was war and turmoil, there probably always will be, but through it all there were those special, simple moments, that I am afraid we have to work hard to find today.

You might be wondering why this book is both a memoir and a book on minimalism. I started by writing just the memoir. Several years ago, Liz McLauchlin, a dear friend of our family from Childs Park Church, read what I had on written on my story up to that point. She has since passed away. She enjoyed the read and gave me this advice, "polish it and see if the newspaper will publish it." At the time it was more of an article than a book.

She, nor I, had any idea that my memoir would morph into a memoir/minimalism book.

During the time I was writing my memoir, I was also practicing minimalism. At some point, I realized that I couldn't tell one story without the other, so I merged the two.

I refer to myself as an aspiring minimalist because I am not there just yet. I am still honing the skills that I am sharing with you in this book for downsizing and learning how to express with less.

I do prefer less material things, and the intangible things are what I hold dear. People, experiences, and memories are what motivate me. I have even written a "happy" list to share with you later in this book.

And although I have kept a few material things from the past and own a few newer things I will need in the future it is the now I am trying to cherish. I hope that I have the right balance in my life, and don't burden myself with excess baggage, be it tangible or intangible. I want to enjoy what I have and live my life unencumbered. Therefore, I've jumped on the minimalism bandwagon.

A DISCLAIMER

Even though I talk throughout this book about "less being more," I do have a disclaimer to make: Being a minimalist doesn't mean you need to take a vow of poverty. You do not need to give away all your worldly possessions to call yourself a minimalist.

You've heard this before, in several ways, and here it is again. When thinking about minimalism, ponder the things that bring a smile to your face. The things that make you happy. Keep those things. If there are things that burden you and you don't want or need, then it's time to weed out. It's time to downsize.

As I reach back into the vault of my life, what I remember most are the people I knew, and the experiences I had, not the things. But I will be the first to tell you there are a few "treasures" that I have kept through the years.

I attend a weekly weight loss group, and just the other day, the topic was stress eating. It's a response that is familiar to many of us. When something stressful is happening, we reach for comfort food. And for a millisecond it works. But the feeling isn't lasting. And the remorse sets in.

The same idea relates to buying something to make you happy. Some people use shopping to fill an emotional void caused by stress or boredom. Often called "retail therapy," it lasts for a short time. Then, once the bills come in, the happiness wains. The key here is the "why." If you buy something to try and fill a void, it won't last. But, if you buy it because you love it and enjoy it, that's a whole different story.

My husband Roger an excellent example of someone who only buys what he loves. As a minimalist himself, he is not a big consumer of things. But the one exception s motorcycles. He loves them. Up until a few years ago, when he got the diagnosis of Parkinson's Disease, he always owned a bike. It brought him great joy.

Even my mother, when she was alive, she would comment about Roger's love of motorcycles. She envied his commitment to the sport. He was forever washing and waxing his bike.

The point here is not to let the term "minimalism" fool you. You can still have things, but once you embrace minimalism, you will find even more joy in what you do own. You will become a discriminating buyer. Everything you possess will either be because you love it or it is something you need.

In the end, you will own a few unique things and not a ton of things that own you.

As you read further, you will realize that being a minimalist does not mean you get rid of everything. There are certain "material things," both large and small that do indeed please you. There are things that you thoroughly enjoy. There are other things you need for day to day living. Of course, keep those things. There will be plenty more to toss out.

CHAPTER ONE

What Is Minimalism?

Minimalism. According to the Merriam-Webster dictionary, the word minimalism has four syllables. Some pronounce it with five. None-the-less, pun intended, it's a movement that's been around for a while. In the many dictionaries of which I have checked the meaning of minimalism, it varies slightly from book to book. But I think the author Joshua Becker describes minimalism best. He states, "Minimalism is the intentional promotion of the things we most value and the removal of everything that distracts us from it." I like that simplistic explanation.

Minimalism speaks to each of its followers in a slightly different way, but in the end the idea of living a simpler life is the same.

I respectfully acknowledge those who are not minimalists, and I make no judgments. I say "summ cuique," "to each his own." But I must assume, because you are reading this, one of three things. Either you are intending to become a minimalist, or you are already a minimalist, or you are a member of my family. So, for whatever reason you are here with me in this book, I am sharing with you my own experiences with minimalism. And imparting what I have learned along the way. I know I am still a work in progress.

What started as two books, a memoir and a book on minimalism, has merged into one. After writing parts of both, I realized minimalism has always been an underlying theme in my life. It just took time to "materialize." Funny choice of words, I know, for an "aspiring minimalist."

I think it is essential for me to know how I came to be this aspiring minimalist. Novelist James Baldwin wrote, "Know from whence you came. If you know from whence you came, there are absolutely no limitations to where you can go." So, in sharing with you're the back story of my road to minimalism, I can move forward with it in a positive way.

In Junior High, my most valued material possessions were my four-inch photos taken with my Brownie camera, my scratchy cassette tapes, that I recorded of friends and family, along with the tape recorder. I still have those tapes today but not the tape-recorder. I have had most of the recordings transferred to CD's, but as yet haven't gotten rid of the originals.

I also had a portable record player and albums from groups like the "Beatles" and "The Association," and soundtracks from "Camelot" and "Man of La Mancha," among others. I don't have the record player anymore, but I do have the albums.

Most anything that I have kept from childhood in the way of material things has a story behind them. They mean something significant to me. They make me smile. Those little treasures that hold substantial memories are things I keep.

The tchotchkes that we have all bought without giving it much thought are out. You might think they are small and don't count, but they add up and begin to hinder us.

I have never really put great value in most material things, but as you will learn when you read further, I went through a "gathering stage" as so many of us do in adulthood. Once you are a gatherer, if you don't rein it in, your things will begin to multiply quickly.

Some might have thought that my grandmother Cordia Cook was a gatherer. And I suppose in certain respects she was. I've even been known to say that my Grandma Cook saved everything. However, certain aspects of her life were minimalistic.

Case in point, I heard my mom say to my Grandma Cook once, "Would you like another piece of pie?" and my grandmother's reply was, "I don't need another piece." She had made that decision thoughtfully, with respect to what would be best for her health and well-being.

All of Grandma Cook's choices were well thought out, and she did nothing to excess. She and my granddad, Ralph Cook, moved to Florida in 1925. They bought a very modest wood-framed house on the south side of town, built in the same decade. There was no air conditioning. The wood floors had area rugs. And from the front porch to the back door was a straight shot which made for excellent ventilation back then. Her home had three bedrooms and one bath, but probably only about 800 square feet. However, it was lovely.

My Grandparents house years later after it had been sold. That's me looking in the window.

Being a product of the Great Depression of the 1920s and 1930s, my grandmother was a very frugal woman. She and

MY GRANDMOTHER COOK'S HOUSE YEARS LATER

granddad Cook had a small inheritance, and they used that wisely to buy a second house to rent out. It was a smart move.

For the forty-plus years Cordia and Ralph lived in that house, my grandmother made more soap from grease she had saved than anyone could count. She used the guavas from the trees in her backyard to make guava jelly. Her neighbors were the happy recipients of much of that soap and guava jelly. She beautifully sewed most of her clothes by hand as well as many outfits for her grandkids. Grandma Cook searched out fabric bargains at Webb City, (tagged at the time as the "World's Most Unusual Drug Store") and the Five and Dime.

Never did my Grandma leave a room that she didn't turn the lights out. Something I do obnoxiously today.

Grandma Cook wasted nothing. She even boiled water for her bath. When I was a little girl spending the night at her house, I thought she boiled water for my bath because she didn't have a water heater. I wasn't any the wiser until I grew older. She just thought she was saving money by boiling water for her bath.

If I went to Grandma Cook's for a visit and wanted to draw or color, she would give me a paper bag as my canvas. That was re-cycling before its time.

Minimalism comes in all forms. My Grandmother Cook was an example of one.

My grandmother's house was neat and tidy. And she knew how to save a buck. But, at the same time, she did have dressers full of scraps of material, thread, string, buttons, and more items that she used in her

MY GRANDMOTHER COOK

sewing. The keyword here is "used." Those things had a purpose. She never spent to excess, overate, or bought things she didn't need or want.

So many people hear the word minimalism, and they immediately think only of material items. They forget that everyday life choices are also a part of minimalism. It truly is a mindset.

My grandmother Cook's philosophy about living has stuck with me to this day.

My mother, not surprisingly, had many of the same traits as my grandmother, her mother. She was a great cook, a terrific seamstress and managed the household pretty much the same as her mother.

I learned by example, the value of a dollar and to appreciate things. Whether it was the blue bicycle, I got for Christmas when I was seven years old, or my little 1950's record player with my 45 rpm records of "The Beatles," I took care of my things. And I was happy with what I had. I didn't pine for more.

Through watching the way our parents and grandparents lived, my siblings and I learned what things were most important in life; family, friends, respect, and a love of learning.

Yes, we had material things, but they didn't hold the value that the intangibles held. So, it seems that I have always had a bent toward minimalism. Right? Not exactly. I was minimalistic in my early years, but as you will read, I strayed from the movement, only to come back to it even stronger. In the following chapters, I will share my journey with you.

Please keep in mind what minimalism looks like to me and what you perceive it to be could conceivably be different. The core concepts will be similar, but how we get there and how we practice it could be worlds apart.

For example, if you and I bought identical homes, I dare say in one year they would not look the same. Maybe you would paint your home white, while I would paint mine pink. Perhaps you would tear out a wall, and I would add a wall. You get the idea. We would have started with the same blueprint but tweaked it to our liking.

Minimalism isn't a cookie-cutter idea. You can make minimalism your own. You and I will probably end up with the same beliefs, but how we get there might be different.

I've read several books on minimalism, and I have always walked away with new inspiration. You might think, "if you've read one, you've read them all," but that isn't the case. Even though the theme of downsizing and living a simpler life is the same thread running through most, each one is as unique as the author of the book.

While I don't claim to be an expert on the topic of minimalism, I have been working at it for nearly a decade. I have had lots of hands-on experience with the movement and want to share that.

Maybe, just maybe, something I have written will resonate with someone and help make their lives just a little bit better. Perhaps this is the fifth book they have read on the subject, and it will be the one that will inspire them the most or maybe not. Either way, I hope that someone will glean a new perspective on the minimalist movement. Maybe something within these pages will make them have an "ah-hah" moment. And perhaps be a positive influence on their journey to living with less while ultimately having more.

I hope that someone is you.

CHAPTER TWO

Bogota, Columbia, April, 1969

A memoir is meant only to tell a portion of one's life. A memoir/book on minimalism might have a slightly different bent. I have chosen to highlight my teenage years and touch on my adulthood, all the while infusing my minimalist approach to life.

My parents had four children.

MY FAMILY LEFT TO RIGHT STANDING: ME, MY MOM, GARY, SITTING: LEFT TO RIGHT SUSAN, MY DAD, LINDA

I was the "baby." I had two older sisters and an older brother. In the spring of 1969, I was fifteen, my oldest sister Linda was twenty-four, my next oldest sister Susan, was twenty, and my older brother Gary was seventeen. We were close siblings and always loved and looked out for each other. By this time, Linda was married and living on her own. Susan was in college and living in the dorm. That left just me and Gary living at home with our parents and my Grandmother Cook. I was a sophomore at Boca Ciega High School, and my brother was a senior. My parents, Jim and Carol Cunningham, thought the sun rose and set in their children, and that is how they raised us.

The world was so different when I was a teenager. No one had a cell phone, so the climate of the neighborhood was different. Instead of texting your friends back then, you picked up a landline phone and called. Or just met at one another's houses and talked. Or you listened to records with your friends. And best of all, you rode your bike around the neighborhood. No one I knew worried about being abducted or worse.

Drive-in movies were in vogue during the sixties as were scavenger hunts, road rallies, super-slides, and progressive dinners.

For those younger readers who are wondering, a progressive dinner was one in which a group of people went to each other's houses for different courses in a meal. The first house would serve the appetizer, the second one the salad, the next the main course and finally at the last home there was dessert.

The good part of the culture of the day and innocence of the sixties is a time in history that I am afraid society will never visit again. The bad part of the sixties; the discontent, the fighting, the bigotry, unfortunately, is still going on today as well as discrimination.

It has gotten so bad today, in 2019, we see fences built around all the schools, with gates that are locked, and the security officer in place. If you choose to visit a school while in session, you must enter through the only entrance, the front door. From there you will find a "teller type" glass wall. You must state your business and show ID. Should you be coming to a conference with your child's teacher, the teacher must escort you to the classroom. There are monthly security drills in addition to the usual fire drills. That is society's "new normal." I accept that there is no other choice, but I don't want the past forgotten either. And it makes me sad that the world has come to this.

Unfortunately, there is no turning back now. It's safety first, and I get that. But I grew up in a time where schools were an extension of the home. Where a child could go to the school playground after school hours and swing on the swings, play basketball, or slide down the slide. No questions asked. Not so today. Once the last bell rings, and the school door is locked, no one is allowed on the school grounds. Times certainly have changed.

Most people feel that the teenage years are the formative ones. I have to agree with that statement. During my teen years, I made a lot of memories, formed my values, and learned about life. As a teenager growing up in the mid-sixties, I lived in the time of the controversial Vietnam War, the protests against it, and the racial riots. At the same time, the famous "Beatles" singing group was promoting peace and love. "Keep on Trucking," was a famous slogan of the day. "Hippie" was in; crew cuts were out. It was a time of change and mixed emotions.

But it was also a much simpler time in many ways. I want to illustrate that point by sharing with you a few stories, of my life growing up in the sixties and relate them to my journey with minimalism.

Stepping back in time to April of 1969 seems like both a lifetime ago and just like yesterday. I was fifteen years old, still about six months away from turning "sweet sixteen," and I was a sophomore at Boca Ciega High School. I played the flute and was in the marching band due in large part because of my wonderful mother.

It was iffy as to whether or not I would even be able to get into the marching band because, to be honest, I wasn't that good. But I knew it was the year that the Boca Ciega Band would be taking a big trip. And I so wanted to be a part of that. I didn't even know the destination as yet. I just knew I wanted to go.

So, with the help of my mother calling the band director, Mr. Dean, and promising that I would take private lessons, he agreed to give me another chance to try out again for the marching band once I completed my tutoring sessions.

My mother was on the shy side, so for her to call the school and talk to the band director was huge. But my parents did all they could do to assure their four children were healthy, happy and well-educated.

I did take the lessons, got better at playing the flute, tried out again, and this time I made it. Shortly after, I learned that the band was going to Bogota, Columbia. A place I had never heard of before. It was outside of our country, and I would be flying for the first time. I was feeling exhilarated.

It is interesting to note it wasn't just the Marching Band going on the trip. The band director was including all of the band groups.

In preparation for the trip, the band sold over sized chocolate bars and fertilizer, as well as held car washes to defray the $160 cost per person. A hundred and sixty dollars was a lot of money in the sixties, but much less than it would cost for the same trip today.

Everyone going on the trip had to get one shot and a passport. The whole process was unusually easy by today's standards.

We were all given a three-page typed list of expectations. I still have that list today. (I have to interject here I don't keep every school paper that has ever crossed my desk, but there are a few treasures that I do hold on to, and this was one of them). And I am glad I have this list because it was such a sign of the times. It speaks to the simplicity of the day.

First of all, the expectations were typed on a typewriter, not on a computer. We didn't have computers as we have today. After being typed, those pages were memo-graphed for general distribution.

Secondly, the expectations were direct and straightforward.

Among the directives, the boys were to wear a dress shirt and tie on the airplane. The "ladies" were NOT to wear shorts or pants at any time.

According to an article printed in the "St. Petersburg Times," chronicling Boca Ciega's Trip to Bogota in 1969, the band members were to be "St. Petersburg goodwill ambassadors." The band would even present a key to our city, to the President of Columbia.

As the time neared for taking off to Bogota, the band vigorously learned the Columbia National Anthem and readied themselves by learning other music as well.

At home, my mom was sewing for me a lovely flowered print, chambray dress with a full-length, navy blue jumper-type over-coat. The outfit that I would wear on the plane. I couldn't wait for the big day.

April 5th,1969; I remember it as a flawless, beautiful morning. I put on that flowered chambray dress and navy-blue overcoat, which felt as crisp as the morning air. My mom was such a great seamstress.

I grabbed my suitcase and flute in one hand, and my band hat and newly dry-cleaned uniform that was slipping off its wire hanger, in the other and plopped them in the car.

I talked the whole way as my mom drove me over the Howard Franklin Bridge to the Tampa Airport, which was about a forty - minute drive. My dad would have loved to come, but he was working, selling cars. And when you sell cars, you don't get a lot of time off. Upon arrival at the airport, we saw the two chartered planes ready for boarding for the long airplane ride to South America.

Tampa Airport in 1969 was a fraction of what Tampa International Airport is today. There were no shuttles or fancy terminals. If you were taking a flight, you just parked in the parking lot, walked through the one-story building, then literally walked outside to the plane and the portable stairs.

If memory serves me right, the flight was about six hours. I googled the time it would take to fly to Bogota, today, 2019, and learned that it is now a three-hour and fifty-four-minute flight. I suppose you would say that is progress.

Full of excitement, but not fully knowing what to expect, I hugged my mom goodbye and with band uniform and flute in hand, I boarded one of the two chartered planes bound for Bogota,

Columbia. On my way to the most memorable five days of my high school career.

LEFT TO RIGHT:
NANCY KING, ME

Soon after I was seated with my assigned band partner, the stewardess approached the front of the aisle to inform us that there weren't enough seats in the cabin and they needed three people to volunteer to ride in the cockpit.

Without hesitation, I volunteered. Two other girls volunteered as well.

Once in the cockpit, we met the pilot, a handsome well-groomed Columbian and his co-pilot, equally easy on the eyes. Hugo, the pilot's teenage son, was also on board. Hugo was a smaller version of his dad.

I was thrilled to be in the cockpit of the plane. I mean, who gets to do that?

As the plane readied for take-off, the only ones sitting were the pilot and co-pilot. Hugo and I, plus the other two volunteers, were standing as the aircraft took flight. We held on to a pole in the middle of the cockpit. With an exhilarating 180-degree view of the sky-blue waters of Tampa Bay, it was a feeling and a sight, I will always, always, remember.

Once in flight, we ended up sitting on someone's suitcases. We talked and sang. At one point the pilot's put the plane on autopilot, and we all sang a loud rendition of Guantanamera. The co-pilot had a giant ring that he tapped on the pole to keep time with the music of our voices.

Hugo and I hit it off right away. It didn't matter that he spoke mostly Spanish and I spoke only English. Meeting and conversing with someone, where both people don't speak each other's language too well, is fascinating. And we were having a blast.

We all talked, laughed heartily, slept a little, while sitting on those suitcases, and at one point, the pilot even let me sit in the pilot's seat. I didn't touch anything as the plane was on autopilot at the

ME IN THE PILOT'S SEAT

time. Again, something that would not happen today. It even seems surreal to me, to this day, that it happened. But it did.

When we got close to the Andes mountains,

the pilots flew higher and then down again when we got to Columbia. One delight after another.

It was dark when we landed at the airport in Bogota, Columbia. I was awestruck at being in a foreign country. Before we headed to "customs," somehow in spite of the language barrier Hugo and I arranged to for him to meet me in the lobby at the Hotel Dann the next day, which was a Sunday. He would be my tour guide through that beautiful city for the next four days.

As band members, we had an itinerary, and assigned rooms, but when we weren't performing "our time" was just that, "ours." There were suggestions of tours or places to go, but we were on our own. I dare say given the same trip today would not afford the kids so much freedom.

It isn't a stretch really to talk about minimalism at this point, because a considerable part of minimalism is the idea to have experiences versus things. And for my fifteen-year-old self, this was the ultimate experience!

After customs, it was a short bus ride to our lodging, the Hotel Dann. The interstate was much like ours in Florida, except for the mountains all around.

When we reached the Hotel Dann, there were

lots of well- dressed Columbian men outside, ready to chat with a North American. That was pretty much the case through the whole visit.

During the next four days, we performed at a local news station, an outdoor amphitheater with a gorgeous backdrop of the beautiful Andes mountains, the University of Andes, and a military academy.

In my free time, Hugo and I walked up and down the sidewalks, all over the city of Bogota. A city framed by beautiful mountains, pretty flowers, and exciting people; like the man who was selling doughnuts stacked on a broken tree branch. I admired his tenacity, but I couldn't bring myself to try one.

The weather was perfect. It was cold enough for my navy-blue trench coat. Being over-cast lent itself to the feeling of surreal. There was magic in the cool, crisp, sweet air.

Hugo and I stopped in a park to have my shoes shined by some enterprising boys, about ages nine or ten. They made my black, Patton leather's sparkle. I think they got a kick out of meeting a North American.

The Bogota Gold museum was a fun stop. It had gold dating back 500 years and was most impressive. There are currently 34,000 pieces of gold belonging to the Inca Empire housed in the museum. I don't know how many pieces of gold they had in 1969.

We took a chair lift up the side of the mountain. A very docile cow and more band members greeted us at the top.

Meeting Hugo's mother and another family member at his house, was interesting since they didn't speak any English. All I can say about that is, smiling is a universal language, and we did plenty of that.

During some of my free time, Hugo and I did a little souvenir shopping. I hung my purse over my shoulder, and Hugo carried my souvenirs and my camera. That very primary Brownie camera where the film goes in the back and the flashcube sits on the top. This camera had documented most of my life up to this point. And would continue to do so as Hugo and I strolled up and down the brick streets of Bogota.

MY BOGOTA SOUVENIRS

For souvenirs, I bought a classical Columbian

album, a small stuffed Columbian doll, a wooden pitcher, and a pair of maracas. I still have everything but the wooden pitcher. Yes, those are among my treasures.

Thinking about that camera makes me realize why it took me so long to embrace digital technology. I like to call it the "Nostalgia factor." I am going to coin that phrase one day if it hasn't already been. It means that one is so attached to something from childhood that they can't embrace a newer technological version.

At every venue where the band played the people loved us. They seemed to be enamored with North Americans. We were like celebrities. I do remember being told though, that the people of Bogota were Americans too, so we shouldn't refer to ourselves as "Americans." We should use the term North Americans.

My favorite place to perform was at the outdoor amphitheater. The amphitheater was free to all the people, and thousands of them came to listen - Adults and kids alike. The seating was just grass and clay dirt as best I can recall. What I do remember distinctly, was the cheering when we played the Columbia National Anthem and even louder when we played our National Anthem.

Against a backdrop of gorgeous mountains, the experience was perfect. The amphitheater enhanced our sound, and we did sound amazing.

I have a picture of two little girls in a primitive, makeshift swing made of tree branches. They were listening from a little further away. It's a poignant picture of a simple life.

It seems like we had barely gotten to Bogota before it was time to come home. Five days went so quickly. I remember what we had to eat the last night at the Hotel Dann. I thought I was eating ham, but later found out it was cow's tongue. It was reasonably good but had I known what I was eating I probably would have skipped it.

After dinner, we packed our bags and prepared to leave the next morning.

Saying goodbye to my new friend Hugo was sad. We exchanged addresses before we left. (We did write for a while and then as pen pals often do, at some point we stopped writing).

Sitting at the Bogota Airport, waiting to head home, we quickly learned that one of

THE AMPHITHEATER IN BOGOTA

the two planes had mechanical problems. That meant one group of people would leave on time, and one group would wait for the second plane. They took volunteers for the first plane. I opted for plane number two. Guess I wasn't quite ready to leave this wonderland yet.

Later I would learn that my parents had driven from St. Pete to Tampa three times to pick me up. There was no communication to parents as to what was going on. Remember this was 1969. No cell phones. No way to notify them. And we ended up being several hours late. I didn't know at the time that this was a stressful wait for my parents. I later wished that I had volunteered for plane number one.

While we waited for our plane, the chaperones passed a yellow writing tablet around for everyone to sign their names — simple bookkeeping for a simpler time.

Many of us slept while we waited for the repairs on our plane. Once they fixed the problem, we boarded, but no one got to ride in the cockpit. Maybe on the first plane, someone did. To this day, I don't know.

Before we took off, the co-pilot was sitting in an aisle seat talking with us, and when he got up, he gave himself the "sign of the cross." That wasn't exactly comforting.

Except for the fire coming off one of the engines as we took off, the flight home lacked the thrill of the flight going to Bogota. They served us some soup but I was too tired to eat.

We all were tired, but that didn't diminish what we were taking home with us in our hearts and minds. We had made new friends, learned new customs, and saw a beautiful country sitting in a valley that spanned 613 square miles. We came home with a pocket full of unforgettable memories.

It's true to my nature to savor the moment, and I was highly aware that this one was fleeting. That indeed, there would be more moments, lots of them. Better ones even. But I would never be fifteen again, in a high school band, on my way home from spending four glorious days in South America.

In this day and age, a trip precisely like we took, would never happen. Security would be so much tighter even if it were a chartered plane. I guarantee no student would get to sit in the cockpit, let alone the Captain's chair. It would be unthinkable. And maybe it wasn't the safest thing to be standing up as the plane took off, but we did it and survived.

The same trip today would not afford the freedom to the students that it did in 1969. And rightly so. The world is a different place.

I am sure that all 111 band members and forty-nine chaperones have a story to tell and I would love to hear them all. It was a magical time for all of us. A time that I will always remember and cherish fondly.

Perhaps you are reading this, and you were a band member back then. Maybe you will share your experiences with me on Facebook. Or pictures. I would love that! Let's keep those memories from fading into oblivion.

As I reflect on this chapter in my life, I am grateful for the experience. I realize that the Bogota trip and all the other experiences I have had in my life, up to this point, define the person I am today: A person who embraces the simple things in life and cherishes each day. A person who is striving to embrace this thing called minimalism.

CHAPTER THREE

Florida Methodist Youth Camp
Summer Of 1969, Age 15

I t was the summer of 1969, and I would be the youngest camp counselor, at age fifteen at the Florida Methodist Youth Camp. Warren Willis, director of the camp, was willing to let me give it a go, after an essay

ME AT FLORIDA METHODIST YOUTH CAMP. I AM STANDING SECOND FROM THE LEFT.

from me and a letter from Jim Dale, the then minister at my church. To this day, I am not sure of the urgency to become a counselor earlier than the norm. But, for whatever reason, I was happy to be on board.

Located in the heart of old Florida, with a backdrop of moss-covered oak trees and Lake Griffin, the camp was a perfect example of how "less is more." A phrase you will repeatedly hear through-out this book.

Each camper, grades seven through nine, attended camp for one week and was allowed one suitcase and, well, that was it. Cell phones and I-Pads or I-Pods or personal computers were not around at that time, so they weren't missed.

Both boys and girls attended the camp. The boy's cabins were on one side of the property, and the girl's cabins were on the other. The girl's side of the camp was "no man's land," and the boy's side of the camp was "no woman's land." End of story. But, to that end, the boys and girls

A CABIN AT FLORIDA METHODIST YOUTH CAMP TODAY. THE SIDEWALKS ARE NEW.

attended all classes, activities, and meals together in a common area.

Now here is where the minimalism comes into this scenario. There was no air-conditioning in the cabins or most of the buildings. The chapel as I recall and the staff office were the only air-conditioned places. Most people didn't have air conditioning in their homes at that point anyway.

There weren't even fans. But with the shade from the trees and breeze off the lake, the heat wasn't a big issue. And for whatever reason, it just didn't seem to get as hot back then as it does now.

There were no electronics in the cabins as well as no rugs, no curtains, nothing on the walls.

Anything the camp lacked as far as amenities, was made up for in laughter, song, and friendships.

Reveille was played at 6:30 A.M. each morning. Up with the sun, we hustled to the bathhouse, brushed our teeth, got dressed, and came back to the cabin to clean it before breakfast.

We had a check-list of things to do. As one of two counselors in our cabin, I was expected to make sure everything got done. Each girl was responsible for making up her bunkbed and putting her clothes in her suitcase. The girls all took turns sweeping the inside of the cabin, the outside stoop and cobwebs. Sweeping wasn't a chore nor was generally straightening up things because we were part of a group and loved having pride in "our" cabin.

While everyone was at breakfast, a group of team leaders would inspect each cabin and leave a report for the group. It sounds sort of military, but far from it. It was just a way to teach respect, responsibility, and comradery.

There was a schedule to be followed every day. There was class time, a music hour, free time, row-boating, swimming, three meals and a one-hour quiet time in the middle of the day, and chapel at night. To signal the end of the day "Taps" was played over the loud speaker followed by a recording of "The Lord's Prayer."

Excellent cooks prepared each meal family-style, and we ate in a vast dining hall. The food tasted like home cooking. One of my favorites was chicken and rice. It was buttery and savory, and almost like my mom's chicken and rice. The cooks made everything from scratch. Upon entering the dining hall, the smell, whether tasty meatloaf and potatoes or sweet brownies, brought memories of a picnic on a summer's day.

At each meal, there was always peanut butter,

apple butter, butter-butter (not a typo, the butter was just called that), and bread. So, if the meal was something you didn't like, or had an allergy to, you could always have a peanut butter sandwich. I know today there are many people with peanut allergies. I don't understand why peanut allergies are so prevalent today, but I didn't know anyone with a peanut allergy in the 1960s. I don't have an answer for that one.

Each camper had kitchen duty at some time. When you had kitchen duty, your task was to bring the bowls of food to the table or clear the table after the meal. And everyone knew before they dumped their scraps into the garbage, to put the napkins and paper goods in one can and the food scraps in another. The scrap food was then given or sold, to a local farmer to feed his hogs — what a great way to re-cycle the food scraps.

The classes, like bible study and crafts, took place in the morning after breakfast in some of the empty cabins.

When lunch rolled around, we were all ready to eat once more. No one ever went hungry at Florida Methodist Youth Camp. And I never heard a complaint about the food. Ever.

Sometime after lunch, the entire camp observed

an hour of quiet. Again, this is right in-line with minimalism. Taking some time for yourself each day is an integral part of becoming in charge of your life. During this "self" time you can contemplate what is important to you and in what direction you want to go. You can take a minute to evaluate your life. How many of us do this? Or feel we have that time?

But this time was built into our camp life.

And you might ask, what did the campers do for one whole hour without a cell phone or piece of technology?

There were three options. Take a nap, read a book, or write a letter.

Wikipedia defines reading as "The complex cognitive process of decoding symbols to derive meaning." I love those three words, "complex, cognitive, process." What a super activity for the mind!

And looking up a formal definition of writing, Wikipedia says, "a written, typed, or printed communication, especially one sent in an envelope by mail or messenger."

Writing a letter sent in the mail has become all but a lost art. It has been replaced today by email. Nothing wrong with email, but there is just something magical in getting a handwritten letter, in the mailbox.

During these summers at camp, the letter was alive and well. It was a fun thing to send and receive mail. Even though the campers were only at camp a week at a time, there was mail call every day.

I mentioned there was free time built into the day. One choice during this time was to join into a simple, yet extremely fun and inclusive dance we all learned the first day of camp. The name was: Mayim, Mayim, which means water, water. It is a popular Israeli dance, danced to the song of the same name. It's a basic dance and one that anyone can join in, at any point of the music.

The dance starts in a circle with all persons holding hands. They do the grapevine step to the left, then walk to the middle and back, then drop hands and walk four steps to the right. Then begin all over again.

The whole idea was that if you are walking by and feel like joining in, you are welcome. It was a simple yet highly effective social activity that was all-inclusive.

Another option during free time was taking a walk down the Path of Silence.

This was just as the name implies. A

human-made path, maybe three hundred feet through trees and brush. At the end of the path

were wooden backless benches and a homemade cross where the sand met the lake.

THE CROSS AT THE END OF
THE PATH OF SILENCE

On the walk, and once you got to the benches, no one talked. It was another chance for quiet in an otherwise busy, bustling day and a chance to re-group before the afternoon sing-a-long.

Yes, every day included a group sing-a-long. Three team members, Waite Willis, Angelo Fuster, and Bob Gibbs, were three very talented singers and guitar players who led the singing. Waite Willis was the camp director Warren Willis's son. These three singers made a couple of albums under the name of "The Rainbow Trio." They taught the campers' fun, interactive songs like "Kookaburra," and "Bring Me a Little Water Sylvie."

Every time they sang "Bring Me a Little Water Sylvie," someone would bring them a glass of water. The singing was infectious, and the laughter was immense. And the songs were ageless.

Before I leave this chapter about my experiences as a camp counselor, there is one night in that summer of 1969 that I must highlight. It was the night of July 20, 1969. A Sunday. The campers from the previous week had left, and the new group would arrive the next day.

I remember the night vividly. As I walked back from the wash house in my flip flops, nightgown, and robe, over a basic "public address system," came the words, "man has landed on the moon." Those words stopped me in my tracks. Of course, I knew all about it, but hearing it like that, in the dark, was startling. The first manned mission to the moon had landed. I had to let that sink in for a moment. The year was 1969, and human beings had landed on the moon. That was astounding. The biggest space event I had ever known just took place.

Looking up through those mossed covered oak trees, I saw the moon and chills ran through me. The juxtaposition of what it took to put a man on the moon and the simplicity of me standing on earth in my rubber flip flops was a moment that is etched in my memory forever.

The plain, no-nonsense cabins, the thoughtful idea of peanut butter sandwiches as a substitution meal, writing letters, reading, talking, singing and joining in a group dance at random, all define minimalism to me. It is the idea that the most significant experiences can come from the most unlikely of places. And that minimalism embraces all these experiences over things.

CHAPTER FOUR

Wometco Crossroads Theater
- May 1971, Age 17

A part-time job does not necessarily shout minimalism. But I would be remiss if I did not mention this part-time job because as you will see, there are lessons to be learned. Lessons that do relate to the art of living smaller and less encumbered.

Day to day life was much slower and less complicated about five decades ago than it is today. I know because I was there. I lived it. If society could take a few lessons, from the old playbooks of the twentieth century and slow down their motors just a bit, perhaps it would work for all of us. It's not going to happen. I know. But I'm just saying, what if?

When I was fourteen, my family moved to a new neighborhood on the northwest side of St. Pete. Our new neighbors, the Foster's lived directly behind our house.

Bill Foster, the dad, was in the business of making orange blossom perfume while Dot Foster, his wife, was the manager, at the time, of the Wometco Crossroads Theater.

My mother and Dot were acquaintances from St. Petersburg High School. It was a coincidence that they ended up as next-door neighbors. The two rekindled their friendship, and Dot came to our house and visited on occasion. Sometimes Dot would have in hand some of her sweet calamondin jelly for us to savor. She made the jelly from the calamondins she picked off her tree. And my mom would return the kindness by making her cookies.

My mom always enjoyed Dot's visits. Both women were intelligent. Both of their husbands were in World War Two, so they had that in common and the fact that they both went to St.

Pete High School at the same time. My mom had four children, and Dot had one son Billy, who was born the same year as my brother Gary, in 1951. Dot and my mom both enjoyed cooking and sharing recipes from time to time — a nice, neighborly relationship.

After I turned seventeen, I decided to look for a new part-time job. I had experience with volunteering at the Florida Methodist Youth Camp. And previous work experience working at the Y.M.C.A. day camp in the summer, as well as babysitting jobs. I was now ready for a year-round part-time job.

The Crossroads theater was literary about a mile from my home. I knew that Dot Foster worked there, so I decided to try and get a job as a cashier and concessions worker.

I talked to Mrs. Foster, my neighbor, and got the job. I must have filled out some paperwork, but not what is required today. There wasn't a computer

application to fill out for sure. And I didn't need a resume' of work experience, volunteering, awards,

THE WOMETCO CROSSROADS THEATER

etc. touting my qualifications for the job. It was a simple process.

The theater started as a one movie theater and later became two.

Another bit of trivia: Right beyond the ticket booth, there was a turn style. Patrons would walk through the turn style after they purchased a ticket. There would be a count of the number of people for any one night. This fact is essential as one night my numbers didn't add up. More about that in a moment.

There were two ushers, an older gentleman Rudy, and a younger kid. Besides ushering, they also swept up the popcorn after the movie.

During the summer months, all of the employees pitched in to help sweep the theater after the kid's movies on Thursdays. Kids are known for being quite messy with their popcorn. There would be popcorn in the seats, under the seats, and in the aisles! But we enjoyed having the kids at the theater.

My job was relatively easy. Beyond the weekly summer movie clean-up from the kids, the job consisted of selling tickets at the ticket window, then making and selling popcorn at the concession stand, along with filling the coke dispenser with syrup and selling cokes and candy. Anytime I'm in the grocery store today, and the popcorn machine in the deli is whirling around, that buttery smell takes me right back to my popcorn making days.

Popcorn and cokes were thirty-five cents each. A movie ticket cost $1.50. Thus, one coke, one popcorn, and one ticket to the movie would cost around $2.20. Not enough to break the bank and very easy on the math calculations.

Compare that to today with an average movie ticket costing around $12.00, and one coke and one popcorn costing $6.00 each. You have a total for one person's theater-going entertainment, at $22.00! A far cry from the 1971 cost coming in at $2.20. It was much easier on the wallet for a date night back then.

I loved my job. People were coming to a place to be entertained and have a bite to eat at a reasonable price. They were happy to be there, and we were delighted to serve them. It was a win-win.

There were three of us girls with the same job, and two of us worked at one time. The other two girls attended St. Petersburg Junior College, where I started that Fall. They brought homework to do during our "downtime."

After the patrons purchased their tickets and

concessions, we had some free time to read or sneak a peek at the movie that was playing.

Many times, we would sit facing the northwest and watch a most elegant, stunning orange, yellow, and red sunset, and daydream about our futures. We repeated that scenario many a night. It was a chance to relax and ponder. Something a minimalist always relishes.

Occasionally, our daydreaming sunset world would be interrupted by a patron wanting a coke refill during the movie, and we would gladly oblige.

Back in 1971, the movies came on large format tape. Each film would have several reels. One day I got to go up to the projection room and see how it all operated.

The movie reels were probably three or four feet in diameter. When it was about time for the reel to be switched to the machine sitting next to it, a small red light appeared on the movie screen. The projectionist flipped a switch, and the moviegoer was none the wiser. The movie continued without a hitch.

Fast forward several decades and today the films are distributed in digital format. I am sure it's much more tech-savvy but also costs more.

I mentioned the turn styles that automatically

counted the patrons. One night we came up fifty cents short. That didn't seem like a big deal to me. But, I guess, in retrospect, every penny counted and accuracy was necessary. I wanted to pay the fifty-cent shortage and go home. But we stayed late and counted money until we found the error. It was a good lesson learned. However, I'm not sure I would feel any different about it today. I would probably still want to pay the fifty cents. Math was never a significant interest of mine. And that amount of money seemed trivial. But I do get it. A business should be accurate.

"Two-Lane Blacktop," "On Any Sunday," and "Red Sky at Morning" were the movies shown during my time at the theater. They were good movies.

"Two-lane Blacktop" was about a cross country road race starring Warren Oates, James Taylor, and Dennis Wilson. "On Any Sunday" was a documentary following motorcycle enthusiasts and racers. Steve McQueen was in that one. And finally, "Red Sky at Morning," starred Richard Thomas and told the story of an adolescent boy and his mother sent to New Mexico while his father goes off to fight in World War Two.

My favorite of the three movies was "Red Sky

at Morning." Really for the soundtrack. It is a mix of instrumental songs and popular songs of the "forties." I own the record album "Red Sky at Morning," which today they call "Vinyl." I liked it that much. The instrumental tracks were melodic and memorable. It was performed by an orchestra with piano music, by Billy Goldenberg. Music that when you listen to, transports you to your "happy place."

When I stop for a moment and analyze my part-time job at the Crossroads theater, I take away the following observations.

First of all, the cost of a night of entertainment in 1971 for a couple's night out was less than $5.00. Even with wages being less back then than they are today, that was still a bargain.

Secondly, I feel fortunate to have worked at such a pleasing part-time job. I sometimes wonder where I would choose to get a part-time job today if I were I that young girl now. I am positive that even a job at a movie theater wouldn't be the same. I wouldn't be allowed in the projection booth and a multi-screen theater wouldn't have the same vibe as a single screen one. Plus, I am sure I wouldn't be watching the sunsets and daydreaming about the future. For a part-time job today, I would probably choose to work in a library. Sorry, the politically correct word now is "Media Center."

As an aspiring minimalist, I would like to replicate the simplicity of this moment in time.

CHAPTER FIVE

The Bear Den Campground
Summer Of 1972, Age 18

It was the spring of 1972. I was eighteen years old. My two older sisters and my older brother were all married and living on their own. I was the last sibling still living at home.

I took a notion I wanted to work at a family campground where my parents had taken me on vacation, just one year earlier. The name of the campground was: The Bear Den Campground.

It was outside of the town of Spruce Pine, North Carolina which was about twelve miles away.

Framed by the Blue Ridge Mountains, with an elevation of 2,890 feet, The Bear Den Campground, at mile marker 324, was and is a picture to behold. Located in the Pisgah National Forest area, people come from all over the country to pitch their tents, hook up their R.V.'s or park their trailers and camp for a while. Today they even have cabins.

I got the okay from my parents and wrote to the manager, Leonard Pack. I explained who I was and that I wanted to work at the campground with my friend Debbie Friley. I proposed that two females would be able to manage a campground as well as any male. Up until that time, mostly males managed the campground. The exception being the manager's wife.

My letter must have struck a chord with Leonard because shortly after I mailed that letter, Debbie and I had a summer job. I felt like I had blazed a trail for all women. I was proud!

By chance, my parents had a small trailer about six feet by twelve feet, and they were willing to let Debbie and me use it for the entire summer. The summer of 1972.

My brother Gary and his wife Angie took Debbie and me to Bear Den in May, and we stayed until August.

During those months, Debbie and I had many duties. We had to learn about the different types of campers and make sure we placed each guest in the correct area. We were in charge of the camp  store, which meant checking in new campers and selling groceries at the small convenient type store, along with keeping the store clean, sweeping, and mopping daily. (To this day the smell of Pine cleaner brings back sweet

DEBBIE ON THE LEFT, ME ON THE RIGHT, IN THE BEAR DEN CAMP STORE

memories of The Bear Den Campground).

Along with tending the store, we also had some outside responsibilities. We pumped gas and sold chopped wood. We made bundles by stacking the wood between two stakes in the ground. If memory serves me correctly, the stakes were about two feet apart and two feet high. Just enough wood for a nice campfire.

Some male employees cut the wood and placed

it in the shed, did the garbage duty and bulldozed new campsites. So, I can't say that we did it all.

For our work, we were compensated with fifty dollars a week and a free campsite. Not bad for a couple of teenagers in the seventies. Two years after that summer, I found two checks that I hadn't cashed. Back then, when we were working at the campground, we didn't have anything to spend money on except food. I thought it was comical, and I called the manager and told him I had found the checks. To my surprise, he made good on them! Again, this was "back in the day."

My parent's trailer worked out perfectly for Debbie and me. It opened up to two beds, one on each side and two cabinets. A small table sat between the beds. It housed my record player. We each decorated our cabinet with pictures we had taken. On my side, the photos were in straight lines, and on Debbie's side, she had a random configuration. A show of our personalities.

Our campsite included a wooden picnic table. We adorned our "dining table" with a striped, terrycloth, table covering. In the middle of we kept a short vase with freshly picked wildflowers. Those flowers that we sometimes picked when we walked down the hill to get our mail. Our digs were "campsite" chic.

What we ate, we bought from the camp store and an occasional trip to Spruce Pine. Mostly we

ate pop tarts for breakfast, spam sandwiches for lunch and hotdogs or box macaroni and cheese for supper. And way, way too much junk food!

ME NEXT TO THE BEAR DEN MAILBOX WITH DAISIES IN HAND

As with all campgrounds, there was a shower house that we had right at our backdoor and slightly down-hill. Perfect until it rained and then we had to be prepared for a red clay mudslide! I did that once and ruined my white "Bear Den" jersey.

Not far from the camp store was a pond — a place for the campers to swim.

We had all the amenities of home. A place to hang out and sleep, a lovely shower house, and there was a laundry on the property as well. We even borrowed the manager's Volkswagen once in a while.

Once we took the V.W. to Spruce Pine and then drove up to Linville, North Carolina. I had a cousin, Stan, who lived there at the time and he worked at the Eseeola Lodge & Golf Club. He invited us up to visit. The lodge has been in existence since 1892. To say it is exquisite would be an understatement. The lush, green grounds just exuded peacefulness. We spent the night there and ate dinner at the hotel.

During that "field trip," we also visited Beech Mountain and a place called "The Land of Oz." The Land of Oz was a small re-creation of the yellow brick road and the trees that lined the path. Located at the top of the mountain, "The Land of Oz" was accessed by a chair lift or buses. We used the chair lift. Once at the top, we followed the yellow brick road to the shops and museum that housed one of the last remaining pairs of the "ruby red slippers," that Judy Garland wore in the movie, "The Wizard of Oz."

Outside of the museum were benches where patrons sat and watched a re-enactment of the last scene from "The Wizard of Oz" movie: The great wizard is getting ready to take Dorothy back to Kansas when Toto jumps out of the "hot air balloon." Dorothy follows him. The wizard then takes off in his balloon, which is a mock-up of an air balloon that is attached to a wire and takes the "wizard" back down the mountain. "Glinda, the good witch" comes and tells Dorothy to click her heels and repeat "There's No Place Like Home." At which time a puff of smoke appears, and Dorothy is gone. For the seventies, it was a cute production.

I googled "The Land of Oz" to see if it was still there some forty-six years later. I found that it is, indeed there, but privately owned now. It is only open on a limited basis. Very limited. According to their website, it is opened every Friday in June and three days in autumn. In 2018 the chair lift access was closed due to renovations. The only way up the mountain at that time was on a shuttle bus.

Another memorable "field trip" was going to see the "Brown Mountain Lights," which were a series of ghost lights reported near Brown Mountain, in North Carolina. Reports of the lights in 1922 determined they were from autos or trains. However, right at that same time, there was a flood and electrical power was lost, but the lights continued to appear. We got to witness those lights, and though they were spooky in a way, we found them fascinating.

During the summer, several family and friends visited. Debbie had a boyfriend visit who brought along his friend. Our friend Betty Williams (Smith) also made it up to the Bear Den. My sister Susan, her husband Jim and his sister Kim came up, as well as Debbie's mom and dad. My parents were our last visitors, who came up to stay a couple of days before taking us home.

You might be wondering what all this has to do with minimalism. But here is the correlation:

First of all, our living quarters were extremely minimal as were the number of clothes we had with us. We couldn't bring many clothes, because we didn't have very much storage space. We didn't own a car, but had access to one should we need it. Of course, we didn't have cell phones. No one did. They weren't heard of yet.

Second, our meals were not costly or fancy, but certainly adequate.

Third, our pay wasn't much, but again, it was enough. We were paid fairly and didn't need much money to live.

And think about the experiences we had. The people we met, the side trips we took, and how we were able to share this experience with family and friends.

My summer at "The Bear Campground," was a most memorable one. Yes, "memorable" is the keyword. You will hear minimalists speak about "making memories" and "moments." Because without being tied down with material things, minimalists make room for moments.

At the campground, we didn't have a huge house to clean. We didn't have to constantly down-size. And we weren't worried about unwanted "stuff." We didn't have stuff. We had the necessities and very little else to encumber us or take up space physically or in our minds. We lived in the moment. We were practicing minimalism and not even aware of it.

But it was perfect, right down to the daisies on the picnic table.

CHAPTER SIX

La Grange College – Fall 1973, Age 19

Shortly after coming home from "The Bear Den Campground" in August of 1972, I went back to St. Petersburg Junior College for my second year.

Nine months later, in May of 1973, I graduated from St. Petersburg Junior College with an associate degree.

In August of 1973, my parents drove me to "La Grange College," a small, private, Methodist school, in La Grange, Georgia. The same Debbie who worked with me at The Bear Den Campground, came along to see where I would be going to school. She was going to college at Florida State.

Packing all of my possessions in the family Ford Fairlane, along with myself, my best friend Debbie and my parents, we took off for La Grange College. My blue bike was in a rack on the back of the car.

Once again, I traveled light. I took my clothes, record player and my few albums, which included "Man Of La Mancha," "The Carpenters," and "The Beatles. I took my notebook, pencils, pen, and that old brownie camera. And, of course, my portable cassette recorder. I also brought a small trash can and some posters for the wall. And the funniest thing of all that I brought with me was a tabletop hairdryer. The kind you sit on a table. Silly to think of that now, but we didn't have portable hair driers. The bike that I brought I am sad to say I never rode. Too many hills!

I remember almost down to the last blouse, the clothes I packed. My mother made most of them, and I love that fact. My suitcase held a seersucker mid-length dress with white polka-dots. (It is important to note the length because in the early seventies there were three acceptable lengths of dresses and they had names: the mini, the midi, and the maxi). Self-explanatory.

Along with that seer-sucker dress, was a printed red scalloped blouse, a solid pair of red, cotton, palazzo pants, a pair of brown checked long pants with a matching jacket, a Raggedy Ann shirt, a blue cotton shirt, a white cotton shirt, pink shorts, a white top with pink trim, a blue skirt and a navy-blue body shirt and a white body shirt. For shoes, I took three pair: chunky heeled sandals, tennis shoes and closed-toed shoes. And I took a coat. It did get cold in the Fall and Winter.

La Grange College had a wonderful, beautiful, hilly campus. The red brick buildings complimented the theme of a small, close-knit school of about 700 students. I chose this college because of the small size and lovely campus. And I thought it would be fun to attend college out of state.

My major was elementary education. I had wanted to be a teacher since I was in elementary school. I loved all my teachers at Childs Park Elementary, where I attended, and though I wasn't a straight-A student, I knew my teachers liked me as well. I could tell by the way they interacted with me. In elementary school, I, along with my friend Debbie, would go back after school was out for the summer and talk to the teachers. Sometimes the teachers would let us help box up books or clean chalkboards. Many times, they sent us home with scraps of construction paper or extra worksheets.

My third-grade teacher was Mrs. Eve. Mrs. Eve was a gray-haired, excellent, no-nonsense teacher. One day she was keeping the class after school for an extra five minutes for being very talkative. There was no busing back then so teachers could keep you after school. Being young and naïve, I raised my hand and contended that my parents would be worried sick should I not arrive home precisely at 3:10. At eight years old, I truly believed what I was saying. Mrs. Eve agreed to let me leave before everyone else. A kid doesn't forget those kindnesses.

I have enjoyed writing poems since I can remember. In High School, I penned poems instead of using my vocabulary words in sentences. And my English teacher Mrs. Moore loved them! She even wrote in my yearbook about them; "Nancy, I've surely enjoyed your poetry this year - Lots of luck, M. Moore." There were so many teachers that I could write about who have positively influenced me. Mrs. Eve and Mrs. Moore were just two among them who showed kindness and compassion and compelled me to want to be a teacher.

So here I was at La Grange starting my new venture. My dorm was, in a word, "quaint." The floors were linoleum tile, and each room had two iron beds that, sitting end to end, were the length of the room. There were two small, metal desks placed at the side of each bed. Most everything in the room came in pairs. There were also two tiny, tiny closets with two built-in dressers separating them and two windows. The only thing that came as one was a mirror over both dressers. It's a good thing I didn't bring too many clothes as there would have been nowhere to put them.

Our dorm was a female dorm only. The male dorm was across the grassy hillside outside our windows.

If a male entered the dorm, you were instructed to yell out, "man on the hall!" No joke.

The showers were halfway down the hallway. A phone booth was a few doors done from my room. Yes, we had a phone booth. There were no cell phones back then or personal computers. We used a landline phone, and we either handwrote our papers or typed them on a typewriter.

College students today would find my college life much different than theirs. It was different, but oh, so good.

We were assigned roommates in 1973. Nowadays, you can find your roommate in a computer search. But I was assigned a lovely roommate Linda Reeder. We didn't see much of each other because she was usually in the biology lab studying. So, I hung out with other girls in my dorm. I was closest to Nalta Parmer Massey.

She and Jane were in the room next door. Jane was dating Terry, so we didn't see much of her. The other members of our little group were Susu, a girl with a golden heart, Sandra from Atlanta who I hitched a ride with a couple of times to go to the Airport, and Deborah, our Southern Belle. There were a

NALTA ON THE LEFT, ME
ON THE RIGHT

couple of guys who became members of our little group. Not boyfriends, but friends. Ted who had the thickest southern accent I have ever witnessed and Mark, who was from La Grange and also spoke with a heavy Georgia drawl. I was the odd man out when it came to accents. Even Nalta had a Southern Accent. Nalta's parents lived in La Grange, but she was staying in our dorm.

Those students made up the group that would sit outside our dorm and talk for hours on end.

We also took a few "field trips." We went on a picnic once in the Spring, saw "The Way We Were" in town, and even took a trip to "Underground Atlanta. When I got engaged to Roger, they took me to a lovely restaurant that served the food family style.

We didn't even have a T.V. in our room. There was a "community" T.V. on the third floor, but we were on the first floor and never watched it. I mean, never. For the eight to nine months, I was at La Grange. I never watched television. Instead, I did something amazing. I talked to my friends all the time. We would spend hours, and I mean hours, sitting on the steps between the women's dorm and the men's dorm in the evening and talked. We joked and laughed and spoke of our futures. It was an unforgettable time.

The college showed a movie about once a week. Not a DVD. DVD's were also not invented yet. But a reel to reel movie. The film I remember most was "The Prime of Miss Jean Brodie." A beautiful story, starring

LEFT TO RIGHT: NALTA, MARK, DEBBIE, LARRY AND TED ON A PICNIC

Maggie Smith, who won an Oscar for her role in the movie. It was about a girl's school in England. The famed poet of the day, Rod McKuen wrote the theme song, Jean.

Sometime during the first week at La Grange, the president of the college invited all the new students to his home, which was within walking distance of the campus. His house was a lovely, older home, and very stately. In the living room, which so reminded me of my Grandmother Cook's 1920's living room with wooden floors and the charm of an English cottage, was a new plastic kiddie pool, filled with gallons and gallons of ice cream. All flavors. And of course, there were toppings of every kind and sprinkles. It was a memorable "make your sundae" affair. A friendly welcome to La Grange College. Another "moment" in my collection of memorable moments.

We were cultured as well at La Grange. Some of the students at the college performed the play, "The Night Thoreau Spent in Jail." A story based on Thoreau refusing to pay his taxes because he didn't want to support the Mexican/American war to which he was opposed. The performance was both professional and riveting.

Another time, a four-string quartet played in the

Chapel on campus. The music was a formidable backdrop for the two impressive stained-glass windows, made in Belgium more than one hundred years ago, that graced the Chapel at La Grange College.

The atmosphere at La Grange College was both kind and inviting. The Methodist Church of the city of La Grange was just up the hill from the campus. I think they adopted us. I remember a covered dish one Sunday held in our honor. It was reminiscent of the days at my home town church, Childs Park, in St. Pete. They had similarly covered dish dinners, and all the dishes were homemade. There were squash casseroles, broccoli casseroles, sweet potatoes with marshmallows on top, crispy fried chicken and potato salad, a buffet too long to list. Set out on long rectangular tables, I can close my eyes now and smell the savory, spicy and sweet tastes of all of that food.

And when exam time rolled around the ladies from that same Methodist Church, brought all kinds of cookies and brownies and desserts for us to enjoy.

I remember one day at La Grange, coming back to my room after eating in the cafeteria. My roommate Linda was sitting on one of the fold-out metal chairs that accompanied our metal desks. My record player was on the other metal chair and my album "Man of La Mancha" was slowly spinning on the turntable. It was on the last song. Don Quixote was about to die, and he was singing "The Impossible Dream." Tears were streaming down my roommate's face. It was a moment I will never forget. Even then, the simplicity of it all hit me. You don't need a great sound system to illicit such a profound response. Today many people opt for the biggest, loudest, most current technology available. And yet, here is an example of low tech, high emotion, and how minimalism can manifest itself.

Being such a small student body, on Sunday's students could visit the cafeteria kitchen and order an omelet anyway they chose. It was something different from the usual weekly breakfasts. It was a small thing with a significant impact.

At some point, my friends at LaGrange College nicknamed me mom. I think it was because I seemed to be the only one who could hem a pair of pants. Or maybe it was because someone paid me to do their laundry. (You do crazy things in college). I'm not sure, but for whatever reason, the nickname "mom" stuck. I haven't thought about that in years.

Being a small student body, our classes were small. The professors were awesome. Being my third year of college, I was now able to take more courses toward my teaching degree; music for the child, math for the child, physical education, psychology classes, and even did my first internship at a local elementary school. Anyone could sense the professors loved teaching.

Dr. Leety, my music for the child professor, was full of sugar and spice. She made us laugh and appreciate how important music is for children. We laughed more than sang. The building where that class was held had older, wooden floors. It very much reminded me of my elementary school.

After two quarters at La Grange, I headed back to St. Pete. My future husband Roger was there, and I missed him. Though I thoroughly enjoyed my time at La Grange, it was time to come home.

I know from looking on its web page that La Grange has grown and changed. There are new buildings and the population has grown. I suppose that is progress. But, for me, I will always cherish that little, un-pretentious dorm room and that small, close-knit group of friends along with those un-ending conversations.

I remember La Grange as one of the simplest, most uncomplicated, times in my life. All the possessions I needed or wanted fit into a small, unassuming dorm room, built for two. The experiences I had were plentiful. I didn't think about minimalism then but was experiencing it one-hundred percent.

The world has changed and continues to evolve. We can't go back in time to the 1970s or '80s or '90s. Nor do most of us want to do that. And, if we don't want to be left behind, we have to change too. But there are choices we can make as we go along, to live the life that is right for us. And to make it as simple as we want.

CHAPTER SEVEN

The Gathering Years - Adult

As an adult, I often think back to my trip to Bogota, Columbia, being a camp counselor at Florida Methodist Youth Camp, my job at Crossroads theater, the summer I worked at "The Bear Den Campground," and my time spent at La Grange College.

I "traveled" light back then. Thinking about that little trailer in the mountains and my quaint dorm room with the tiny closets, I realize I had everything I needed or wanted. I wouldn't have changed a thing.

On December 22, 1974, the happiest day of my life, I married Roger Hoffman. Our wedding was like other weddings in the seventies. Even though I had five attendants, it was much less complicated and less expensive than weddings tend to be today, but I wouldn't go back and change a thing. I often have remarked that I would do it all the same way again.

ROGER AND I AT OUR
WEDDING RECEPTION

In the 1970's it was customary to serve cake, punch, and nuts at the reception. No buffets or sit-down dinners for hundreds of people. I have never embraced the way of sharing one's wedding as they do today. I guess it's up to the individual, but for a minimalist, that's too much.

Our modest ceremony was at Childs Park Methodist Church, my home church. The guys rented tuxedos, and the girls in my wedding party wore long, red, satin dresses. Roger and I each had five attendants.

My sisters Susan and Linda were bridesmaids,

Roger's sister Lisa was a bridesmaid, my niece Julie was a junior bridesmaid, and my buddy from Bear Den, Debbie, was my maid of honor. Ushers were my brother Gary, my cousin Mike, a friend Fred, and Roger's brother Joey was the best man. And our three-and-a-half-year-old nephew John was the ring bearer.

The bridesmaid's dresses were hand-sewn. My mom, sister's and Roger's mom Iva all had a hand in that. Not being a seamstress, I didn't know that the material I picked out was difficult to sew. But no one complained, and the dresses were flawless.

I prided myself in finding my perfect wedding dress at a small boutique shop on Central Avenue for only thirty-eight dollars. And I loved that dress. It was off white with a high neck, long sleeve, full length, and no train. Very simple. It had a Cummerbund at the waist. It was the best.

The veil cost more than the dress by a few dollars. It was white with lace, and my mom had to dye it off white to match my dress by putting it in hot tea.

I opted for red and white carnations for my bridesmaids and a white bouquet for me. It was December, so the church filled with several red poinsettias, which cut down on the cost of flowers considerably.

We were married without the fan-fair of weddings today, and it was lovely. I would not go back and change a thing. Rev. Dale, the minister who I spoke about in the prolog of this story, performed the ceremony along with Rev. Albury, the current minister. We asked that the marriage passage from the book "The Prophet" by Kahlil Gibran, be read.

Our honeymoon was in Inverness at my parents' little cabin in the woods. We fixed our steak dinner and enjoyed the peaceful surroundings that the woods afford.

OUR WEDDING ATTENDANTS LEFT TO RIGHT: LISA, SUSAN, LINDA, DEBBIE, JULIE, REV. ALBURY, ME, ROGER, JOE, FRED, GARY AND MIKE

Returning from our honeymoon, we set up housekeeping at Colonial Oaks, a one-bedroom apartment in Kenneth City, Florida.

At $125 a month, it was a good deal. That's what a decent apartment, in a good neighborhood, was going for in the seventies.

Today for the same apartment it would probably go for $800 at least.

Setting up housekeeping, we had the usual shower and wedding gifts of towels and sheets and kitchen things to begin our new married life.

I brought with me what I like to call memorabilia: pictures, cassettes, some of my first-grade papers. I also had books. There were Yearbooks, college books, and lots of miscellaneous stuff.

As I already stated, my husband Roger was quite the opposite. He had some photos from the Navy, his duffle bag, harmonica, and guitar. He has always been a minimalist, and I so admire him. Roger's mom told me that when he was little enjoyed watching other kids play with his toys. A mark of the minimalist, he was finding joy in simple things.

Now that I was out on my own and married, I slowly began to acquire even more things. I enjoyed going to garage sales and stocking up on tchotchkes and anything I could get for a bargain.

I didn't necessarily spend a lot of money. And that is an excellent point to make here. You can become a collector of things without much money, especially if you like thrift stores and garage sales and bargains.

Very soon after we were married, I got a job teaching elementary school, and Roger got a job at the county as a civil engineer.

Getting a job as an elementary teacher might as well come with a disclaimer to be prepared to start an extensive collection of teacher-made and bought games and other teaching tools to assist you in the job. I know because I taught school for thirty-two years. It starts with one box and grows. I can't think of a teacher I have met who hasn't acquired a multitude of teaching aides, boxes of games and "tubs" of stuff. It just "comes with the territory," as they say. But this goes against what minimalism stands for.

I may write an entire book just for teachers. There needs to be a manual for new teachers on how to deal with the multitude of games, books, puzzles, "manipulatives" and other "extra" enticing media to keep their students engaged. Especially for Kindergarten teachers. And it is a challenge to house and catalog this stuff. As I said, that will be another book.

Once again, I refer back to my childhood. The look of the classroom was so different. So simple.

In my fifth-grade class, for example, there was a bulletin board on the back wall with the three branches of the United States government displayed.

THE BEGINNING OF MY
SCHOOL BOXES

Some books sat on a small shelf on the north side of the classroom. There was a chalkboard in the front (along with the teacher's desk), and four or five rows of student desks. That was your typical classroom. But somehow without a million extra "props" and every square inch of the room filled with some teaching tool, we learned. Unfortunately, teachers have little autonomy in their classrooms in the twenty-first century.

Married with new jobs we hadn't settled into one dwelling as of yet. For the first nine years of our marriage, 1974 to 1983, we moved quite a bit. Each time there was a different reason for the move. When you are young, your reasons for moving are not always the same as when you get older. For example, when we were younger, we moved once to get a dog and then again because the dog kept climbing the fence. We found a house that had a fence that the dog couldn't climb. And we flip-flopped from preferring to rent a house to renting an apartment.

Fast forward thirty years. One of our reasons for moving involved having not such savory neighbors. Your thought process completely changes as you age.

During that decade from 1974 to 1983, we lived in seven rentals and bought and sold a house. And I gathered things. The thing I had not learned to do yet, was to get rid of something old when I got something new. That is a number one strategy for a minimalist. So, my stuff just kept piling up.

In 1984, Roger and I bought a home for the second time on eighteenth Avenue North, in St. Pete, Florida. It was just a few blocks from my parent's house.

OUR HOUSE ON 18TH AVENUE NORTH

Our new home was only eight hundred square feet, the perfect size for a minimalist. It had two small bedrooms with teeny-tiny closets, a small living room, a kitchen, and a room off the kitchen where we ate our meals.

There had been a wall unit air conditioner in that eating room that had been taken out. We put a fish tank in that space. It was really outside the box. Extremely artsy. That was my husband, the artist's, doing. He is truly a renaissance man. Very creative, artistic, and just plain "artsy."

At this point, I had shed a lot of my baggage just due to so many moves. And in retrospect, I didn't have nearly the "baggage" I thought I had at the time. It wasn't until years later that I would learn what it was like to have much more stuff than one can handle.

Roger re-did both the kitchen and bathroom. He put cedar boards on the walls of the bathroom, and our backsplash in the kitchen was faux brick.

We had central heat and air put in, and siding put over the shingles. It was a picture. We loved it, and it was a minimalist's dream home.

But then life happens. About one year later, on Christmas eve, my father died of a sudden heart attack. The week after was a blur. Our extended family came, and it was a sorrowful time. We had the memorial, and a few days later everyone went back home.

Roger and I started staying at my mom's house after my dad died to help take care of the house and be there for my mom. Her large ranch style house was going to be too much for her. The three of us brainstormed the possibility of finding another home with a mother-in-law apartment. We searched in the area with no luck. There might be more of those today, but in the eighties, there were none to be found.

So, we continued to live with my mom. We decided to sell our little minimalist house on eighteenth avenue north, the one my friend lovingly dubbed "The Gingerbread House," and make my mom's home our permanent home too.

About two years later, we all decided to add a second story to my mom's home, where Roger and I would live. It would be kind of like an apartment. It would have a kitchen, living room, bathroom, and bedroom.

We met with the contractors to decide where the stairs would go inside the house. There would be a small upstairs deck with outside stairs. We talked about the kitchen, bathroom,

THE SECOND STORY ON
MY MOM'S HOME

living room, and bedroom. The kitchen would be more for snacks as Roger, and I ate our meals with my mom.

The addition turned out beautifully, and for the next twenty-three years, that is where we lived.

We put all of our furniture from our tiny house upstairs.

Downstairs housed the furniture my mom and dad had purchased, along with furniture my mom had inherited from her mother.

In 1968 when my family moved into that house, my Grandmother Cook still lived in the house she had lived in since 1925. In 1970 my Grandmother Cook moved in with us and brought her furniture which included two huge armoires, a desk and a bench made by my grandfather Cook, another antique desk, two antique chairs, a couch, quilts, hand-made pillows, and many, many other smaller items.

During the time that Roger and I were with my mom, we hosted numerous family get-togethers, both large and small. We had plenty of bedrooms and enjoyed when the family would gather.

In the years of entertaining family, my mom and I gathered even more things. Almost every Saturday we would go to garage sales while Roger would visit his mom and often do house projects for her.

My mom and I never spent much money at the sales but loved getting pretty knick-knacks, kitchen items, and the occasional end table and lamp. Among the kitchen items were casserole dishes, whisks, glasses, plates, pots, pans, and placemats.

We loved coming home with bags of treasures. But believe me, those treasures multiplied. At one time, I counted eight sets of placemats in the buffet. At that point, I hadn't learned the art of "replacing" instead of "adding to." So, our stuff multiplied.

Being neat people, we were careful to store away our stuff, so it didn't look cluttered, but the cabinets, buffet, and armoires were over-flowing. There were linens, blankets, towels, knick-knacks, antiques, papers, pictures, albums, and holiday stuff. Pots and pans, silverware, and glassware filled every cabinet in the kitchen to the top. We had recipe books, a toaster oven, muffin tins, cake pans, and double boilers. And mirrors. We had a mirror in every room. Oh, and lamps. We had many table lamps, floor lamps, big lamps, and small lamps. No shortage of light in our house!

But garage sailing was our passion. It was time

that Mom and I spent together, and we weren't going to give that up. And luckily or unluckily, depending on your vantage point, we had tons of storage closets in that house. To be exact, we had seven closets, and four built-in drawers below those closets. We also had two large armoires. The kitchen wasn't large by today's standards but still had at least ten deep cabinets. And every inch of those storage spaces was utilized.

In 2007 my mother-in-law Iva was making some decisions of her own about her housing. She had lived alone, in her house in St. Pete for several years after her husband, Joe, my father-in-law, passed away. And she was now ready to sell her home.

Roger had been helping her fix her house up, as well as keep ours in good shape. We invited Iva to come to live with us, and she accepted. Roger helped pack up her whole house in boxes and moved everything into our place. He and I, along with my mom, lived downstairs and Iva lived upstairs.

That meant Roger, and I had to bring all of our "accumulations" from upstairs to downstairs to be stored somewhere. And that somewhere was in one of our many closets. It worked, but we were beginning to feel the effects of having too much stuff. The closets were starting to bulge.

Iva was with us for a year before she realized the stairs were too much for her. She decided to move near her daughter and family, and her other son and his wife, who all lived in Longwood Florida. She ended up moving to Apopka, Florida, which was fifteen minutes away from them. So, once again, Roger helped her pack up, and Iva made another move. And we took lots of our stuff and carried it back upstairs. We kept the bed downstairs and used that as our bedroom. At the time, my mom had some health issues, and we needed to be where we could hear her, should she need us.

In 2008, shortly after Iva left, I retired from teaching. I wanted to spend more time with my mother, as her health was failing. I had thirty-two years teaching under my belt, so it was probably time to retire anyway.

The next three years were a bit stressful. Roger and I cared for my mother and tried to make her as comfortable as possible. I took her for rides in the car and played her favorite Danny O'Donnell tapes. We would often drive through McDonald's and order a milkshake. She didn't have much of an appetite, but I could entice her with a chocolate shake. Her primary health issue was her shoulder, but being in her late eighties, she opted out of surgery. She also had mild dementia, but mostly she was sharp as a tack until the end.

In 2010 and 2011, my mother had several falls. She ended up in rehab in the Spring of 2011. After rehab, she went to stay with my sister Linda in Altamonte, Springs, Fl., for a while. She passed away on August thirteen of that year. It was a devastating time for me. I knew it was coming, but no one is ever prepared to lose their parent.

The whole extended family came for the memorial service and it was a fitting tribute. Many family and friends spoke of their fond memories of her.

After everyone went back to their respective homes, it was time for Roger and me to figure out what our next move would be. Figuratively and literally. Our house was now too big for us. We always knew that we would sell that house one day, and now that day was here. It was time to downsize. But where would we start?

CHAPTER EIGHT

Six Moves

It was now September of 2011, and as Roger and I sat in our over-sized, two-story, four-bedroom, three-bath home on a double lot, we contemplated where we would go from here. We knew for a long time that we would sell the house someday. Now that day was here, and the task seemed monumental. But the house was too big for the two of us.

In the middle of the month, we put our house on the market and decided that when it sold, we would rent on the beach for a few months to re-group. We found an apartment complex called Seaside Villas in Gulfport, Florida, that rented short term, furnished apartments. We planned to downsize first, put the rest of our stuff in storage and take it out after living three months at the Seaside Villas. By then we would surely have figured out the rest of our plan.

While the house was still on the market, we put into motion the first part of our plan. It was time to start downsizing. But how is that done?

We had thirty-seven years-worth of stuff. More when you factor in my mother's things and my grandmother's things. What do you keep? What do you give away or throw away? The task seemed daunting. No, it didn't seem daunting; it WAS daunting.

First, we took an inventory of the things that were not sentimental in any way and that we didn't need or want. A day bed, a couch, an overstuffed chair, and miscellaneous lamps went on the shortlist. We called a hauling company to take those things.

Second, we took a look at the things that the family might want and be able to transport. Among these were two desks, a sewing machine table, and two armoires.

And third, the hardest of all was what to do with EVERYTHING that was left! We had to decide what to keep and what to give away. As I have already stated, my husband is already a minimalist. So, he didn't have had any problem getting rid of things. But, me, I wasn't there yet. This part for me was both challenging and cathartic.

When you are forced to take a look at what is important to you, it makes you examine your life differently. I think it was at that very moment I decided that I wanted to pare down things in my life and live a simpler lifestyle. I wanted to become a minimalist.

But I quickly found out that minimalism is much more than getting rid of material stuff. It is the philosophy of living every aspect of your life in a more simple, calm way.

It boils down to what you consider important and essential in life. Whether it be an iron skillet or a T.V. show, or whether or not to take a yoga class or learn to play the piano. It is all about what you know will make your life whole. It's living an uncluttered life in all ways possible.

Lucky that my husband and I are on the same page. Neither of us likes clutter. However,

I am overly sentimental and nostalgic. That's not necessarily a bad thing, but it can get in the way of minimalist thinking. Especially when you have a penchant for saving every sentimental thing you have ever owned in your life.

There is an old sitcom that Roger and I watch probably too much. It is called The Goldberg's. The show is about a family of five; two teenage boys, their older sister, an over-bearing, over-sentimental mom Beverly, a no-nonsense dad Murray, who is often the voice of reason and a grandpa who lives with them. It takes place in "eighty-something." In one episode, the dad Murray is trying to convince his wife "Bevvy" that she doesn't need to hang on to every piece of artwork her children have ever created. As "Bevvy" goes through the box with her children's artwork, she can't throw anything away. She keeps holding up a scribbled drawing or some noodle art or other art her kids have made through-out the years and puts it back in the same box. Murray encourages her to get rid of the stuff. As we were watching that particular show, I sat up and proclaimed, "I AM Bevvy!"

While we don't have children, we do have nieces and nephews, and through the years they have sent us cards or other things they have made. And I have hung on to those. These same nieces and nephews now have kids of their own. It was the perfect time to do something with those items along with tons of other things I had saved through the years.

So, the downsizing began. At first, I would pick up an item, and as I thought about whether or not to keep it, ask myself a million questions. When did I buy it or did someone give it to me? If I bought it who was with me? If it was a gift, who was the gift giver? Will I need it someday? Will it be expensive to replace? I was asking myself all the wrong questions when there was only one question that I needed to ask: Does this item bring value to my life? But to bring it all down to one question is easier said than done. It takes practice and a certain amount of commitment to your principles. It is exactly like the old saying, "you can't have your cake and eat it too." But slowly with the help of my husband, we managed to whittle down our belongings to a manageable lot or so I thought.

It was now time to rent a Portable on Demand Storage unit or PODS. The company was going to bring us a sixteen-foot storage unit. We were to fill it up, and the company would return to pick it up in one week. Then, for a nice little fee, they would store it for the next three months.

Now, here is the funny part. Even after getting rid of the extra couches and the extra chairs and the many odd lamps and side tables and hundreds of miscellaneous things, we quickly realized that one storage unit wasn't going to hold all of our items. We had to get a second sixteen-foot storage unit! That was a shocker to both of us. However, we had no choice at that point. We ordered a second unit. We started putting things in and before long it too filled up. We still didn't have enough storage room, and this was getting ridiculous! I honestly couldn't believe it. I think it is true that you don't know how much stuff you have until you get ready to move to a new location.

So, we packed up both sixteen-foot storage units to the limit and everything that didn't fit we gave away, to our neighbors. And let me tell you they got some beautiful things. Ironically by this time parting with our extra things just got so much easier. At some point, you smile and say, "take it!"

Both PODS were picked up and readied for storage for the next three months. We kept out some clothes and bathroom items, but our fully furnished apartment had all we were going to need.

Shortly after we moved into our apartment, I was visiting my friend Denise Giammarco at Cross

Bayou Elementary School, and she introduced me to the principal. After the principal and I talked a few minutes, she asked if I would be interested in an hourly teaching job. I said "why not" and after a trip to the school administration building filling out papers and getting fingerprinted, I started working part-time as an hourly teacher at Cross Bayou where I had taught Kindergarten in the eighties.

We enjoyed living right on Boca Ciega Bay and taking evening walks to the Gulfport Casino to watch the sunset from Williams Pier. Every Tuesday, they have a farmer's market. Vendors come out and set up everything from tomatoes to jewelry. It is a great venue. Gulfport is a lovely, artsy city, and it inspired the setting for our future children's middle book series, "The Saltwater Kids."

Our furnished apartment was even smaller than our 800 square foot house on eighteenth Avenue North. At just about 600 square feet, it was the perfect minimalist dwelling. It had one bedroom, one bath, a small living room/dining room combo and a little, but well put together kitchen. There was a place in the kitchen that housed a small stackable washer and dryer.

Items that we needed seem to come in fours.

There was eating service for four, four glasses, four coffee mugs, four pots, and four tea towels. The exception to the number four in the kitchen was only one tea kettle and one skillet. There was nothing to excess.

In the bathroom closets, we found four white towels along with four washcloths and an extra set of sheets.

I had to laugh; they even had two empty picture frames on a small table in the living room, ready for my pictures.

The best part of the whole apartment was looking out the sliding glass doors from our couch and seeing sailboats sailing by and sometimes dolphins. It was gorgeous! We were living like minimalists as our "stuff" sat in nearby storage. We were trying minimalism on for size and it fit.

Three months go by fast when you are having fun. The time came quickly to make another decision. Where to go next?

Roger and I had made a few trips to Gainesville, looking at houses to buy, but didn't find one that was a good fit for us. I know we were picky, but after leaving our home of twenty-five years with nothing found wrong by a home inspector except a tiny cracked yellow tile in a window sill, we had high expectations. The more we looked, the less we found. We did love the idea of living near family in Gainesville, but we couldn't find the house that would work for us.

So, for the time being, we decided to find a house to rent in St. Pete. We looked on Craigslist and found a home for rent on eighth avenue north. We moved into the house on April first of 2012. We had our two PODS delivered and began unpacking. Again, we assessed what we had, and once more, made several trips to the nearby thrift store with things we didn't need or want. This list included lamps, dishes, frames, and side tables. Determined, we promised ourselves that when we moved from this house, we would only need one P.O.DS.

We lived in this rental house for a year and decided to move on. It wasn't the house for us. During this time, we did look at homes to buy in St. Pete, but again, came up empty.

In February 2013 we moved on to rental number three on Jungle Avenue North. It was a sweet little house on a lovely tree-lined street. As it turned out, the landlady, Regina and I attended Boca Ciega High School, at the same time but didn't know each other back then. Regina and her husband Jerry were great landlords. And living one street away from Park Street, which was one street away from the intercoastal waterway, was indeed a nice perk.

This time we only needed one PODS to move. We were so proud of that fact until we realized that it took an additional seventeen trips in our pick-up truck to bring all the extra small things to the new home! As a couple, Roger and I hadn't achieved minimalist status yet. We just got a taste of it when we lived in our apartment in Gulfport.

We settled into this house quite quickly. It was a great neighborhood with lots of old trees and friendly neighbors. We got to know the neighbors to our left, John and Karen, a lovely retired couple. We never really got a chance to know the neighbors to our right. I learned from reading my Grandmother Cook's diaries that knowing her neighbors was important to her. She was by most markers a shy person, but she did like her neighbors. Maybe I take after her.

Our family visited during this time, and we even re-connected with our cousins George and Carmela from California. That was a highlight of our time spent in that house, along with the seventieth birthday party we threw for my oldest sister Linda.

During the second year on Jungle avenue, we entertained the idea again of moving to Gainesville. We even found a house to rent there. But we found out that if we moved to Gainesville, my insurance premium was going to go up. So, we decided against leaving the area. Having the itch to move again, we found a rental off twenty-second avenue north and Tyrone boulevard.

This time we were so proud that we were down to one PODS and one truckload. The fact that we were moving so many times made it easier to get rid of things. Knowing that each item we got rid of was one less thing that we didn't have to move was a no brainer. It was a great impetus for downsizing. That stuff gets heavy after a while and cumbersome.

So, we were at four moves by this time, and I estimate about 150 boxes of stuff besides furniture. Remember this minimalist lifestyle is a work in progress. I truly believe if we hadn't of moved so many times, we would still be hanging onto much of what we shed. Thinking about having to move big items and lots of boxes is a grand motivator for getting rid of stuff that you would otherwise have to move.

We stayed in the house near Tyrone Boulevard for a year and a half. In December of 2016, we finally decided to make a move to Gainesville. Our fifth move in as many years. I had a new insurance carrier so we figured it would work out this time. By this time, we had gotten rid of enough "stuff" that we felt we didn't need a PODS. A large moving company would work! Wow, progress! Little did we know.

We hired a small, independent moving company to move us. Roger and I packed up the house. The movers were going to pack up our stuff in their truck and put it in storage for a week.

Then, onto the house in Gainesville. Down to about a hundred boxes, I was feeling good about our progress. We had cut our box count by about a third.

On the day of the move, our movers came to pick up our stuff. We went to the store while they started filling their truck. I was so proud of how much we had downsized. Almost gloating.

But, not for long. When Roger and I got back from the store and running some last-minute errands, the movers were waiting for us. The head mover said to me, "Boss lady, you've got way too much stuff. It won't all fit into this truck!"

Shocked, I reiterated what he had just said, "It won't fit into our truck. Are you kidding me? Really?"

"That's right," he said, pointing to the ping pong table, toaster oven, a small bookcase, and miscellaneous other items still sitting in the garage.

At this point we were tired, and it was getting ready to rain.

Our neighbors behind us ending up getting the ping pong table and my neighbor Laura got a painted shelf for her daughter. We gave the toaster oven, some tools and other miscellaneous to the movers. One of them brought their truck and parked it at the house so that he could store his stuff. The ferns also went to neighbors. One to Laura and one to Gail. Gail called them "Mom Cook's ferns." My grandmother Cook started the ferns eighty-something years ago, and she gave the family clippings from them to start new plants. So, everyone in the family had one of her ferns. I knew I could get a cutting from one of my sisters to start the fern again; therefore, I didn't mind parting with them. And it was a sweet going away gift for our neighbors.

Not quite having achieved my goal of minimalism, we headed to Orlando, our first stop on the way to Gainesville. With our Nissan, packed to the rim and the moving truck squeezed shut, we headed out of St. Petersburg. The moving van went to storage for a week.

We looked like vagabonds with our truck over-flowing.

We spent the next week with my sister Linda and brother-in-law Byron in Altamonte Springs, Florida, before heading to Gainesville.

January first, 2017, we moved into our Gainesville rental. We settled in, quickly finding Publix, Walgreens, the gas station, and Walmart. We changed our driver's license and had cable installed at the house. We got a library card and took a class in sign language. We found new doctors but then discovered that even though I had changed my health insurance, my new insurance was no good in Gainesville either. The nearest city that would take my insurance was Ocala, forty-five minutes away. So, I got a new insurance plan that raised my premium by eighty dollars a month.

I joined Weight Watchers with my sister Susan. She and I enjoyed walking the Mall a few times a week, and I lost a few pounds.

The best part of moving to Gainesville was living close to family. I come from a close-knit family. Roger and I were immediately welcomed with open arms by my sister Susan and her husband Jim along with my niece Jennifer, her family, and nephew Pat and his family. They even had a welcome party for us. But still, we missed our hometown of sixty-five years. It was the place where we both grew up, and, it held all our memories.

After being in Gainesville for about six months, we had a decision to make. Stay or return to St. Pete. After much deliberation and angst, we decided to return to our hometown. Another move. Number six.

In June of 2017, we found a rental house that was just around the corner from the rental we had left six months prior. It had the same floor plane: three-bedroom, two-bath home, on a corner lot.

Of course, moving again meant packing and downsizing just a bit more. We gave some furniture to Salvation Army and lots of small items that we realized we never used.

We hired the same movers who had moved us up to Gainesville, to take us back to St. Pete. They seriously were surprised and impressed at how we had lightened the load. We were down to roughly seventy-five boxes. Yes, I did keep count. And we had gotten rid of our treadmill and our wicker furniture. In hindsight, I probably have not let go of the wicker furniture. But, as you will realize, there will be decisions along the way of this journey, that you might question. It's all part of the process. And that's okay.

As we unpacked our things into the sixth house is six years, I vowed that the next time we moved we would walk out with only the clothes on our back. Okay, not really. But I did vow to become as minimal as was possible.

Oh, and those ferns? Gail, our neighbor, called soon after we moved back and insisted on giving me "Mom Cook's Fern." I did appreciate that gesture and took it back. It is thriving well on our front porch.

CHAPTER NINE

My Goals For Achieving Minimalism

The number of goals you will set on your journey toward minimalism is up to you. There is no correct number. I chose three goals. You might prefer more or less.

There is also no time limit. Again, it is an individual choice.

Whatever the number, whatever the time frame, set your goals, make your goals happen, and finally, maintain your goals.

Yes, we aspiring minimalists all have the final

goal of ending up with less, but the road to getting there will be different for everyone.

For each of us, our way of work will be slightly different, but in the end, we should each feel unencumbered and "lighter."

I attend weekly weight watcher meetings. There is a prescribed program to follow to lose weight. But within the application, there is flexibility to choose the foods that you want to eat. No two people like the same foods, and some people have allergies or food sensitivities. So, everyone's food diary will look different, but hopefully, everyone will achieve their goal of losing weight.

The same philosophy can apply to minimalism.

Your chosen minimalism goals and way of work to accomplish them may be different than mine.

For example, maybe I like down-sizing a whole room at one time — top to bottom. And I want to finish it in one day. Whereas you might choose to tackle only a closet, and you are going to give yourself two weeks. We would both be working toward the same outcome of having more while living with less. But we will get there in our own way and time.

To get you started with thinking toward your

goals for minimalism, I will share my goals with you now.

GOAL NUMBER ONE: TO HAVE CONSIDERABLY FEWER MATERIAL POSSESSIONS THAN I HAD WHEN I STARTED THIS JOURNEY.

Some people are specific about how many items they will keep. I have read, "The 100 Thing Challenge" by Dave Bruno. His goal after downsizing was to end up with just 100 things, counting all underwear and socks as one.

Though sometime I might take Dave Bruno up on his challenge to own just 100 things, I am not there yet. Remember I am an "aspiring minimalist." So, for now, I am working on just KNOWING what I own. This is a challenge too. And since I don't have a photographic memory, I will automatically end up with less stuff, if I want to recall it all.

GOAL NUMBER TWO: I MUST LOVE WHAT I OWN OR NEED WHAT I OWN.

I used to go to garage sales every Friday and Saturday. It's a great way to find all kinds of things at great bargains. But it is also tempting for the minimalist. Today, I will occasionally stop at a garage sale on my way home from somewhere, but mostly I shop at thrift stores and antique shops for entertainment, not necessarily to buy anything. It's like a treasure hunt. I am looking for the diamond in the rough. But I don't buy anything unless I love it or it at least serves a purpose. And, as a caveat, I don't buy everything I love, I love everything I buy. There is a difference.

GOAL NUMBER THREE: IN ADDITION TO SHEDDING MY MATERIAL CLUTTER, I WILL SHED MY EMOTIONAL CLUTTER

Most people think only of down-sizing material things when talking minimalism. They forget about the emotional clutter that takes up space in their minds. Things like worry, bad habits, or obsessions. Sometimes this is a more daunting task than paring down the physical things. But it is worth it in the long run.

So, those three goals sum up what I want to accomplish by living minimally. Three links in a chain. All three interconnected and dependent on the other.

What will your goals be? What will be your strongest link? Your weakest link? Start brainstorming now. Your goals could be similar to mine, or maybe you have different ones altogether. In the next three chapters I share with you some practical solutions that have helped me achieve my goals and maybe they will help you.

CHAPTER TEN

My Practical Solution To Achieving Goal
Number One: Having Fewer Possessions

In every book or article or news story that I have
ever read about the subject of minimalism, it
usually deals with paring down in some way. It
begins with a mindset, and the rest follows.

My mindset is: I know I want to live a simpler
life, with fewer meaningless things and a few real
"treasures." I want to express with less.

If you've read much on minimalism, you've
probably read about the "three boxes" or the "three

bins" or maybe even the "three bags." The idea being you get three containers and sort your items in those. Box one is for things you will throw away, box two is for things you will keep, and box three is to give away. I have also added a box four, the "limbo" box for the items I can't decide where they go.

The box routine is a technique I used each time we made a move as well as times in between.

Box one, the box for throwing things out, is straight-forward. Broken items that can't be repaired, like a broken flashlight, is easy to toss or recycle. Old make-up, pencil nubs, and plastic lids that don't have a matching container are other examples. To me, these things are no-brainers. Anything you can't fix or has no life left in it must go in the trash or recycle bin.

Box number two is for things you want to keep. It is a little more difficult for me. You will need to do some soul searching on this one. You must ascertain if the item is essential to your life or if you love it. Think about how much you value that item. If you know without a doubt that you do love it or need it, then it goes into box two. On the other hand, if you know right away the opposite, you don't want it, then it goes in Box three, the give-away box.

Box three, the give-away box, doesn't need much explanation. In this box, you will put what you are willing to part with and give to someone else. Be it the thrift shop or a family member or friend.

So those are the infamous three boxes. And then there is the fourth box that I have added called the "limbo" box. Sometimes going through your stuff, you might be un-decided about an item. You don't know whether to keep that item or give it away. So, you toss it into the "limbo" box. Then, like my grandmother used to say, you "stew on it" for a while. At some point in the future, like a lightbulb going off in your head, it will become apparent to you whether to keep that item or give it away. It might take a week or a month, but eventually you will know what to do with it. This idea of a fourth box helps with the angst. And you don't have to make that decision right away.

Here is an example of something I put into my "Limbo" box: a shirt that I hadn't worn in a while but I thought I still kind of liked. After a month, I realized that I genuinely didn't care for the shirt. At the end of the month, it was easy for me to move that shirt from box four, the "limbo" box to box three, the "give-away" box.

Things in boxes two and three still have lots of life left in them. It does get tricky trying to sort what to keep and what to give away.

Sometimes you have had things for years. Treasures, I like to call them. And treasures are great if they don't take over your life, but if you aren't displaying them or using them in some way, they are not only taking space up in your house but your head as well. Some of the things are newer purchases. Things that you just had to have and then realized after you bought them, that you never used them.

Here is an example of a couple of newer things that were taking up my space: a small ice cream maker that I bought to make "diet" ice cream. An oxymoron if I have ever heard one. Diet ice cream. I tried making it once, and it was an epic fail. I didn't like having to freeze the canister first, and the ice cream wasn't that good. So, that was easy for me to put into box three and give to the thrift store, along with the juicer that my husband and I thought was going to be better than it was. In the first place, the juicer required a ton of fruit, which is expensive, to make one glass of juice. And secondly, it actually had too many calories. And, thirdly, cleaning the juicer was no picnic.

The lesson to be learned here is before you buy that appliance or exercise equipment, or anything for that matter, think about it first. Ask yourself if you will use it. No impulse buys. Waiting a few days will give you clarity.

A couple of older things that I decided to keep, I put up on a display shelf. One was a sweet, little wooden music box that my dad made for me when I was collecting music boxes. My husband hand carved the words, "Another Music Box" on the top. I will keep this music box along with a plastic egg my mom decoupaged me for Easter one year. And to be honest, I have a shoebox labeled "treasures" that I get out and look at from time to time. Those items are unique, and I love them, and I will keep them always.

I think you will find this four-box method will work for you. It forces you to take a look at each item individually and make that determination. Remember, you are the one in charge.

When sorting my belongings, I do one room, or just one closet of the house at a time, be it the kitchen or bathroom or bedroom because I don't want to overwhelm myself. I usually allow an hour or two for sorting and do it about once a month.

As you get less "stuff," it will take less time to go through. Eventually, it will be like a "maintenance" activity. That's what I am approaching. Honestly, I am getting very close to achieving all my goals. But, until then, I still have a little more work to do.

Everyone's schedules are different. Some of us are working, some not, some retired, all different scenarios. Should you choose to try out this box method of sorting, the time frame is up to you.

Whatever method you use to weed out your stuff, over time you will witness success and it will become second nature.

Keep in mind; it is better to do a little at a time than to get frustrated and give up because you are trying to down-size your whole house at once. That won't work. A chunk at a time will whittle your things down nicely.

CHAPTER ELEVEN

My Practical Solution To Achieving
Goal Number Two: Only Owning
What I Love Or Need

My mindset is, I know I want to live a simpler life, with less meaningless stuff and a few real "treasures." Things that I love. But it is so easy to accumulate things. We all do it. We collect everything from "soup to nuts," as the saying goes. And the thing I collect the most is pictures. In this example of dealing with my myriad of pictures, I will explain how I have dealt with them.

The challenge for me isn't to have absolutely zero pictures, but it is to keep the photos that mean the most to me. The ones I love. And I want to be able to retrieve any given image with a modicum of "looking" for that said picture.

For me, this has been difficult as I am a staunch sentimentalist and that sometimes gets in the way of my minimalist lifestyle. It is hard for me to part with a picture. But I have found ways to deal with that issue.

As you read in the first chapters of this book, with every move my husband Roger and I made we pared down the big stuff and some of the smaller things. I was at an advantage initially because I was on a deadline with each move. That facilitated making some split-second decisions.

But, when there was more time, I had to reach deep and decide what I loved and needed. In this way, I was even happier with the outcome.

So, here is what I did with all the pictures. One day, I took my fifteen or so boxes of four by six images, some garbage bags and a few large envelopes. I sat on the couch to go through them. I will tell you we are talking thousands of pictures.

I labeled a large manila envelope for each of several family members whom I knew would love some pictures. I am fortunate to have a large, extended family. In giving away these pictures to family members, I felt comforted that the photos would still be in the family. I decided to earmark some images for family members that were mostly of themselves and their families, with a few others thrown in that included other family members.

If a picture was blurry or mostly unimpressive scenery, I tossed it into the garbage. And I did throw away some of the hundreds of faded pictures from my teaching days. What I ended up with was far fewer photographs and some lovely giveaways to family members. I have started to organize those boxes by years, which I think is an excellent way to be able to retrieve a photo when I am looking for a certain one.

I still have some five by seven and eight by ten photos to keep or give away.

I know that many of you would scan the pictures and then toss the hard copy. That is an option, but I prefer pictures I can hold in my hand. My mother was that way too. Especially those old black and white pictures.

However, I will say with my cell phone and digital camera I do download my current pictures and that saves them by month. I concede that will work for those pictures.

Taking pictures and doing projects with them is one of my hobbies, so I am at peace with the photographs I have kept and happy that I know where to find a picture when I am creating a photo project.

This is just one example is how I have dealt with my goal number two: loving what I own. You can use my tips to get a handle on sorting through anything and finding what you really love.

CHAPTER TWELVE

My Practical Solution to Achieving
Goal Number Three: Shedding
My Emotional Clutter

Anything that weighs heavily on your mind I call emotional clutter. It could be a habit that you want quit, or an obsession. My biggest emotional clutter is worry.

What does Meriam Webster say about worry? Webster says, "VERB 1. Give way to anxiety or unease; allow one's mind to dwell on difficulty or troubles."

I think those of us who are worriers are born with that trait. Worrying is in our genes. We worry over things that we have no control over. Each of us is an individual with individual needs, so I won't even attempt to delve into anything more than surface emotional clutter. Should you have deeper concerns about what might be your emotional clutter, then please see the professionals for those.

What does worry have to do with minimalism? It's simple. Worry is emotional clutter in your mind that you don't need. It takes up a lot of time and energy. I have come up with a few tricks that work for me to wrangle in my worry.

I have started keeping a paper and pen by my bed at night. If after my head hits the pillow, and I begin to worry, I write down my thoughts. It is a simple tool, but it clears my mind, and I can sleep.

Another way that I try to deal with worry is to talk myself through whatever it is that is bugging me. I think about what I would tell a friend if they had the same concern. Again, that does help.

Taking a walk or some exercise always seems to help me if I have a good worry going on.

And the last thing I do is to keep busy. Maybe I will make cookies or read a book or write on my stories. Those are things that I can do to get my mind off my worries.

I am working on shedding my emotional clutter as we speak. I think that when I get rid of the last tchotchke, I probably will still be working on the "worry" piece. But that is okay. I'm a work in progress.

To recap, my three goals on the road to minimalism are to have considerably fewer possessions than when I started this journey, to love what I own or at least need what I own and in addition to shedding my material clutter, I must rid myself of the emotional clutter.

Those three goals sum up what I want to accomplish by living minimally. Three links in a chain. All three interconnected and dependent on the other.

What will your goals be? What will be your strongest link? Your weakest link? Start brainstorming now. Your goals could be similar to mine, or maybe you have different ones altogether. Remember, it's whatever works for you.

CHAPTER THIRTEEN

Let's Talk Books and Media

Now that you are thinking about your goals I am going to touch on some specific areas of my life where I have learned bucket loads about minimalism. Dealing with books and media is a good place to start.

Should you be reading this and you were born in the nineties, or beyond, VCR tapes and cassette tapes will be foreign to you. And you probably read your novels on a Kindle. So, your media will be much easier to deal with than mine. This chapter is for people who were born earlier, but might be of historical interest to the younger minimalist.

One of the heaviest things to move, besides furniture are books. It is hard to pack them and make the box light enough to transport. When I pack books, I always try to make the box fifty-fifty with half of it containing books and the other half with something lighter like pillows or towels.

I guess I think in terms of moving because I have done it so much. But even if you are not thinking of moving, hardback books and even paperback books take up a bunch of space.

Yes, there is such a thing as e-books. And e-books are great. But what do you do with all those paperbacks and hardback books you already own?

I am not just talking about novels and biographies. There are cookbooks, yearbooks, church directory books, and other sundry types of books.

How does a minimalist pair down the books or media? Where does one start?

I think you start with the obvious. Not unlike the three boxes, you kind of know what books you will keep. For instance, here is what I kept right off the bat. I kept my yearbooks because I do refer to them from time to time. And for me, they speak volumes. Sorry, I am a sucker for puns.

I also kept two unique books Roger purchased for me when we were first married. One is a love poem, and the other one is a fairy tale book because I taught school.

Port Town, Kaboom, The Big Story, and *Adaptations of Technology,* written by George and Carmela Cunningham, my cousins, as well as *Bridge Finders* by my nephew Josh Cook and two books by my friend Debbie Hills Abrahamson, including *Brittany's Big Surprise,* are all keepers. I love and have kept. A few years ago, I transcribed both my Grandmother Cook's diaries and my mother's diaries into hardback books. I will always keep those.

I have a few copies of two picture books, *Amelia's Rainbow* and *Fourth Grader Parker Engels, Poetic Justice,* that Roger and I had self-published about ten years ago. Along with those I have two middle-grade chapter books, *The Saltwater Kids on Boca Ciega Bay,* and *Casting Call,* both of which Roger and I wrote, and he illustrated and were published by the Reader Publishing Group within the last two years.

A Child's Garden of Verses by Robert Louis

Stevenson, given to me by my grandmother Cook when I was seven, a poetry book my brother Gary gave me titled, *To See a World in a Grain of Sand* and a few other select books are ones that I don't want to part with.

Those books are treasures, and I love them.

Next, I will look at each book that is left and individually make a judgment call to keep or to pass on to a family member or the thrift store. Surprisingly I don't have that many more to go through before I have it narrowed down to one shelf of books.

As I have said throughout this book, minimalism is different for everyone. Maybe you will end up with four shelves of books to my one. And for you, that is wonderful because you undoubtedly love those books and will pare down in another area.

This chapter is titled, "Let's Talk Books and Media." We've talked about books, now a little about media.

Besides my books, I have family VCR tapes, commercial DVD's, family DVD's, family CDs, and some cassette tapes from the seventies. That's my "media." Your media may look similar or different.

I have transferred most of my family VCR tapes

to DVD, and I didn't save the VCR tapes. That is a milestone for me. What helped me to let go of the original VCR tapes was the fact that someone told me a VCR tape would only last fifteen years. I have not confirmed that but it worked for me to let go of the old tapes.

When I was in Junior High school, I started audio taping family members and friends using a small tape recorder and little cassette tapes. I ended up with several cassette tapes. Those tapes have been transferred to CD's.

In my hall closet, this part of my media is labeled in a few boxes and categorized by year. I am satisfied with that.

For me, minimalism is not only getting rid of stuff, but having knowledge of what you do own and feeling good about those things. If I can't tell you what I possess then for me, I have too much stuff.

CHAPTER FOURTEEN

What If?

I was thinking the other day about a T.V. show from 1965 called: "I Dream of Jeannie." The show was about an astronaut who, when stranded on a desert island, found a genie in a bottle. Upon getting rescued, he took the genie back to live with him. She granted his every wish.

What if, I thought, I found a magic lamp or a bottle with a genie inside? What if, that genie granted me three wishes? What would those three wishes be? A simple if/then question.

Silly to think about finding a genie in a bottle,

I realize, but still, what if? I know precisely my three wishes. Do you know what your requests would be? All my wishes would hinge on money. That might sound funny coming from an aspiring minimalist, but I want to be honest. My three wishes would be money to donate to research for Parkinson's or other diseases, money to give family and friends and thirdly, money to put into the bank for a rainy day.

But, what if, that same genie put a stipulation on my wishes and demanded that they must be non-materialistic wishes. What would I wish for then?

Putting on a stipulation likes this makes the "exercise" a little more challenging. But, after thinking about it, the following list is what comes to mind. My non-materialistic wishes would be as follows:

First of all, to be able to listen with cat-like ears to what others have to say. Listening might be an under-rated skill. I came across a quote by N.R. Hart that said, "As a writer, you try to listen to what others aren't saying… and write about the silence."

We need to listen to what people are saying

and pay attention to any underlying messages they might be conveying.

A great example of this comes from my late grandmother Cook. When she would get a letter from "up home" Indiana, she would read it cover to cover. Then, on occasion, she would "read between the lines" as she often expressed. Sometimes she would comment that her sister or whoever wrote the letter, was not telling her the whole story. Some might call it intuition. I call it merely paying attention when someone speaks or writes. If you can hone the skill of listening to others, perhaps you will listen to your instincts as well. If you are downsizing and you are having a difficult time, then you need to ask yourself why and listen to your answer. It is easy to not listen to what your head is telling you when your heart is competing with it. It becomes a battle of head versus heart. But listen to both. Each has value. And in the end, you will be able to move forward.

Secondly, I would like to have the in-ate ability to be able to express whatever is on my mind meaningfully, at any given time, to anyone. It would be fantastic to make my words always have meaning for the listener or the reader and never have inconsequential babbling. Or bragging. Or preaching.

This ability would undoubtedly come in handy should someone ask me their opinion about something. It is a gift to be able to offer a viable suggestion to someone reaching out. And conversely, maybe you need to reach out to someone for advice yourself. Perhaps you need a second opinion on your minimalistic efforts.

Part of becoming a minimalist has to do with minimalizing worry, which I have discussed, and living a simpler life. For me, being able to ask for help when I need it or give support when someone solicits it is a big step in living a simpler, less complicated life. The art of conversation is genuinely just that, an art. And to be able to have the right words in any given situation is a gift.

My third and final non-materialistic wish would be to have the skill to make the right decisions easily, be them minor or major.

No more second-guessing. A situation would present itself in which I needed to make a decision, and there would be no problem. I'd make that decision and never look back. Notice I would be specific about wish number three. I want to make the "right" decision. Not just a quick decision.

Of course, this is key to any minimalist. Not only deciding what to keep and what not to keep but everyday decisions at the grocery store or making any purchase, for that matter.

I just went to a shoe store intending to buy a pair of white tennis shoes. They didn't have the shoes I intended to buy. However, I did find a pair of white, sort-of like tennis shoes. I asked myself, "What if white shoes get dirty too easily?" "What if they don't have enough support?" All the questions I should have asked myself before I went to the store. It would have made my shopping experience so much easier. The fact that I needed shoes was not the question this time. The problem was what kind? I needed to come better prepared to make an informed decision.

Maybe you can't decide what to do with an item that someone gave you and you don't have a use for it. You become saddled with the problem of whether to keep it and store it or give it away.

Or maybe you spent a lot of money for that state-of-the-art, free-standing mixer you bought six months ago, yet you have never used it since you first took it out of the box. And now you feel remorse for buying it in the first place. You don't want to keep it, and you don't want to give it away. Have you been there? I have too.

So first you need to come to terms with buying it in the first place. Maybe it wasn't the best choice, but you deal with it now. You can turn around an old decision by making a new decision. The decision to let it go and promise yourself to think things through the next time you decide to make a big purchase. I have had this happened to me many times.

I am never going to come across a genie in a bottle. But this non-materialistic "what if" exercise is a great one for the minimalist because it puts emphasis, not on material things, but the intrinsic feelings going on inside each of us.

And since I don't have a genie granting me the skill of quickly making the right decisions, I will practice, practice, practice that art until I am successful.

Seriously, I don't need a genie to make my wishes come true. I only need confidence in my ability. And then I can make those wishes come true. And so, can you.

CHAPTER FIFTEEN

Dealing with Gift Giving

One of the first ads of the holiday season this year just aired on T.V. Paraphrasing, it said, "It's not how much you spend on the gift, it's time you spend together. A great message, although odd for a retail store when their objective is to make money.

Who knows, maybe they were using reverse psychology? Perhaps they are appealing to our sense of not over-indulging when it comes to gift-giving, while at the same time hoping that the gifts, we do purchase, we will purchase from them.

In all of my research on minimalism, I haven't come across much on the topic of gift-giving.

Somewhat of a challenging issue for the minimalist, gift-giving can be dealt with successfully.

There are many different holidays celebrated each year: some religious, some not. And of course, we can't forget the birthday gift giving. For some people, that might add up to one holiday a month or more. Times when we are giving and receiving, and it is equally a challenge.

I grew up with a Methodist background, and my favorite holiday has always been Christmas. There are so many beautiful traditions that my family celebrated for the season. We baked sweet, mouth-watering spritz cookies, bought a fresh tree to decorate with those treasured ornaments of the fifties, and sometimes even put angel hair or tinsel on the tree. The choir at church would put on a Christmas pageant and our family always made looking at the outside Christmas lights a special event. Living in St. Pete in the fifties and sixties, anyone making the trek out to look at lights wouldn't miss going by "Doc Webb's" house. "Doc Webb" was the founder of "Webb's City," The World's Most Unusual Drugstore."

Beyond the cookies, tree and light excursion, there were the beloved stockings and the gifts from Santa and mom and dad.

Honestly, I loved my stocking better than opening the gifts. There were four of us kids, so four stockings. Our stockings looked like socks. They all had a picture of Santa on the front.

There was always an orange in the toe of our stocking. Next, there were clanking walnuts amongst the small trinkets inside. And finally, there were those miniature chocolate Santa's individually wrapped in colorful foil paper.

My sisters, brother and I would get up before the crack of dawn on Christmas morning. We were allowed to get into our stockings, but not the gifts before my mom and dad got up for the day.

When my parents got up, we started opening numerous presents. We would take turns opening up a gift so we could see what each other got. Santa usually got what was on our list.

At the time, I never considered that we had too many gifts. I was a kid, and it was fun to get presents. I knew a family in the neighborhood where the parents got each of their children just two gifts. I felt so sorry for the kids to be only getting two presents! But, now, my whole philosophy has changed, and I think two gifts are a fantastic idea!

Even though we did get a lot of presents for Christmas back in the fifties and sixties, I think today the whole idea of gift-giving at holidays has evolved into an extravaganza. The gifts are much more expensive and more numerous. I have seen so many times where kids get "bucket loads" of presents from their parents, then more from their grandparents on their mother's side, then more from grandparents on their father's side. Do the kids genuinely appreciate the gifts?

Another point to consider is the fact that many kids get all kinds of things like electronics throughout the year, whenever they asked for something. So, when a holiday like Christmas comes, they don't appreciate it as much as they should.

I remember when I was about four years old, and my birthday rolled around. We celebrated at my Grandmother Cook's house. There is only one gift that I can specifically remember from that birthday. It was a tiny clothesline with tiny colored clothespins to hang up my doll clothes. To this day, I can picture myself sitting on my grandma's porch swing holding that clotheslines with all the little colored clothespins, thinking that it was so cool. I would hope that all kids would appreciate their gifts in that way.

The best gifts, in my opinion, are gifts from the heart. That could include something handmade, a field trip somewhere, or another unique experience. And the best gifts don't have to cost a lot of money, even though it seems that many of our kids and youth of today have considerably more expensive tastes. I believe kids can be taught the value of a dollar at an early age and taught to appreciate what they have and the fact that not everyone is as lucky as they might be.

Some examples of alternative gifts to the "big ticket" items are as follows:

For the very young, handmade gifts such as wooden toys or blocks are often so unique that it might be the recipient's favorite gift. Not all of us have the skills to handcraft a wooden toy, but a good day spent at an antique store might garner the perfect gift at the right price. And there is always e-bay for the unusual gift.

Teenage gifts might be a little trickier. But think about making a gift basket. Fill it with treasures found at a garage sale or thrift store. Add favorite snacks and maybe a ticket to a movie. The point is to buy with purpose and creativity. That will win out every time.

Adult gift giving can be a challenge, as well. But, again, homemade is a true gift from the heart. An offer to babysit or wash someone's car would surely be a surprise gift, wouldn't it? Or, if you aren't able to wash a car, how about a gift card to a car wash? And there are plenty of charities to donate to in someone's name. What a gift of love that would make.

The old saying, "It's the thought that counts," is what I, as an aspiring minimalist, try to embrace. Whether you are giving or receiving it's the same plight. You don't want to hurt anyone's feeling by trying to tell them what or what not to gift you. Acting by example is a good start. I think you might be shocked by the number of people who don't practice minimalism but are envious of those who do. And they would welcome a little nudge toward that way of life themselves.

CHAPTER SIXTEEN

More Strategies Learned Along the Way

Whe thinking about becoming a minimalist or at least becoming minimalistic, it is helpful to have some concrete strategies in dealing with consumerism. Most of us enjoy shopping and even looking for a bargain. But the bottom line is, the item is not a bargain if we don't love it or need it and have space for it. In that regard, take a look at the following three strategies for buying:

STRATEGY NUMBER ONE: Purposeful and mindful buying

I got a text from my friend Denise the other day. She sent me a picture of a lovely buffet type table that she found in an antique store at a terrific price. She was contemplating buying it. Instead of an impulse buy, she took a picture. What a great strategy. She was "buying" herself some time to consider the purchase. It's so easy to talk yourself into having to have "that" item "right" now. Whether it's a big item like a table, a couch, or even a smaller piece.

With this strategy of purposeful and mindful buying, make sure that you have a clear vision of what you want.

I give my friend Denise kudos and tons of credit for not buying that table right then and there. Sure, there is a chance that the table may not be there if she decides she wants it later. However, I have a theory about that.

My theory is, if you can't decide, then deep down you either don't want it or don't have room for it.

Remember Dorothy's famous last lines from The Wizard of Oz right before she admits, "There's no place like home?" She is talking about looking for her heart's desire and relays if it isn't in her backyard, then she never really lost it anyway.

Maybe the thing we are looking for is already in our home, and we don't know it. Perhaps we want a new look and just moving around some furniture, will do the trick.

My husband and I are well known for changing things around in our home. Taking an end table from the living room and putting it into the bedroom and or moving the love seat from the East wall to the West wall. Moving things around might make us seem fickle to some people, but it is a great way to use what you have and maximize your space to the fullest. And to get a whole new look in the process.

And just like "Dorothy," what we want, might be right there under our noses all along. We need to rearrange things to see it. That old saying, "you can't see the forest for the trees," fits here perfectly.

I have heard many times that if you have a decision to make, then flip a coin. The idea being you will know what you want before the coin lands, because while it is in the air, you secretly wish for it to land on a particular side.

Another way to look at this is with a term I learned when I was teaching elementary-age kid's economics. It is called "opportunity cost." For every decision made, there is both an opportunity and a cost associated with that opportunity. Whether in business or personally.

All we have to do is to figure our opportunity cost for whatever we are buying. And by figuring it out, I mean asking ourselves some basic questions.

In the example of my friend and the buffet table she was considering buying, she most likely asked herself these questions: Do I love it? Do I need it? Can I afford it? And finally, do I have a place to put it? That leads to my strategy number two for purposeful and mindful buying:

STRATEGY NUMBER TWO: Ask yourself how much real estate are you willing to give up for each item in your home?

A little over thirty years ago, Roger and I decided to take a real estate class. Though we decided early on, it wasn't for us; we did take away some interesting and helpful information.

Most people think of real estate as being a piece of land or a house. And that is true.

But real estate also refers to space and capacity. Here is an example I remember from real estate school: If you are selling soup in a grocery store, you will want to take up as much real estate in that store as possible so the consumer will notice your soup over the competition.

But in your home, though you are probably not selling soup, you still want to make the best use of your real estate as possible.

You want your walls and the things in your home to be a reflection of yourself. You might have heard the term "Feng Shui," the Chinese art or practice of placing items in such a way to bring harmony between the flow of the environment and that of the user. It is also believed to bring good fortune.

So, as you rearrange a room, you might want to think of how the placement of things affects you.

And whether you own your home or you are renting, you want to consider how much real estate you are willing to give up for each item you have.

There is wall space and floor space. What you bring into your home needs to be put somewhere. Therefore, when you are contemplating buying something, it is helpful to ask yourself, "How much real estate am I willing to give up for this item?

My living room sometimes becomes an issue for me. As an aspiring minimalist, I feel like less is more in all areas. But, at the same time, a minimalist always asks some semblance of the question, "Does it bring me joy?" when deciding to keep an item or get rid of it.

This joy thing is a complex issue. Here is an example: On the one hand, I want my living room to have minimal furniture. On the other hand, having family and friends over does make me happy. And those friends and family need a place to sit.

I remember once, twenty years or so ago, Roger and I opted to use bean bag chairs as part of our living room furniture. My friend Denise was gracious and sat in the chair and said it was cool. But, really, now that I am in my sixties, and many of my friends and family are older, that bean bag chair idea doesn't bring any of us much joy.

It took me several trial and error moments to figure out how I could be minimal and accommodating at the same time. Roger and I finally opted for three chairs and two love seats. And our guests don't have to sit on the floor.

Speaking of entertaining, I have learned a few things along the way about that.

When we were living with my mom, we always had enough plates, silverware, glasses, and cups for as many family members who wanted to visit at once. It worked at the time. But, as you probably know, that means storing those things, and it makes for a major clean up after a meal.

Now, most of the time, we use paper plates and paper cups when we have company. We have as much fun as we have ever had and no one has ever complained. And it makes for easier clean-up. I know that it might seem wasteful to use paper plates, but it isn't that often that we use them. And, again, if that is something you can't, or don't want to do, then don't do it. You will make your blueprint to make minimalism work for you.

The go-to questions are still, "do I love it, and do I need it?" But for larger items like couches, desks, and tables, consider adding the question, "How much real estate am I willing to give up for that item?"

And if you want to live a simpler, uncluttered life, less is more, so keep that in mind, even when trying to accommodate your guests. Remember, too, that some furniture can do double duty. You can always pull the kitchen chairs into the living room for extra seating.

The final strategy I use in navigating minimalism is a game I that I made up called "The Inventory Game."

STRATEGY NUMBER THREE: PLAY THE INVENTORY GAME

Most people, like myself, enjoy a good game. Maybe you like chess or checkers. I enjoy "Scrabble" and also the card game "13." Whatever your game is, you like it because it is fun and challenging, right?

The inventory game is also fun and challenging. It is a great memory game as well as a helpful tool for the minimalist.

If I gave you a pen and paper right now, could you inventory everything in your house room by room without looking to see what is there? Quite the challenge. It is a game that I play over and over, often in my head. Sometimes when I can't sleep, I will play the inventory game.

I came up with this idea because I want to know what is taking up space in my home. I start with the kitchen. I name the things and where I keep them. Admittedly, I don't count every knife, fork, and spoon. But I can tell you in my silverware drawer I have knives, forks, spoons, baggies, foil, and wooden skewers.

If I can't name most of what is in my kitchen, then I need to get rid of something because I have too much. I exclude food because it is consumable. After inventorying the kitchen, I mentally go through each room in our home and the closets to try and recall what is in them.

For example, in my second bedroom closet, next to the bathroom, I can tell you that I have three large white boxes and in those boxes are pictures. And those pictures are categorized by decade. There are also six towels, six washcloths, and six hand towels. I keep a second set of sheets in a pillowcase. At the bottom of the closet, you will find three handmade pillows by my mother, and three or four cut out pieces of a quilt made by my grandmother Cook. On the top shelf is an over-night bag. That's pretty much it.

The distinct take away here is: the less you have, the easier it is to know what you have.

I find this a great mind exercise and a way to take stock of your home and life. It isn't as hard as it sounds, although I will admit, I have been doing this for a while, and I would estimate that I have downsized by at least seventy-five percent.

Recently I decided to purge my clothes closet. I found some small round, cedar circles with a hole in the middle that fit on a clothes hanger. These cedar circles are supposed to keep out moths. But since I had pants in three sizes, I decided to label the circles and hung the clothes by size. Just like in a store!

Seriously! What was I thinking? For weeks, then months, I would open my closet and admire the neatness of my closet. But, during those weeks and months, I only wore one of the three sizes.

Yes, I wanted to lose weight, and I still do, but there is only one size that you or I can wear at one time.

I decided right then and there to get rid of anything in my closet that didn't fit me at the time. I filled a plastic bag with thirteen pairs of pants.

Next, I took a look at my shirts. There were several cute shirts that I never chose to wear. In the bag, they went.

My closet now only houses clothes which fit me, and I like. It is so uplifting to only have in my closet those items that I can and will wear. As a bonus, I found a pair of pants, that fit, that I hadn't seen in weeks.

I think these three strategies of purposeful and mindful buying, thinking of the real estate in your home and finally, playing the inventory game, should you choose to try them, will be helpful in your minimalist journey.

CHAPTER SEVENTEEN

My Biggest Hurdle

Paper "stuff" is my nemesis. It is that s i m p l e. It's my biggest hurdle.

It's relatively easy for me to part with kitchen things. I don't mind scaling down on bath towels. With encouragement, I can part with my tchotchkes, trinkets, and baubles. I could probably tell you all the clothes that I have in my closet now that I have cleaned it out. And the side tables aren't dear to me. But, when it comes to anything in the paperwork realm, I am sunk!

I think it's a throw-back from my childhood. I

have vivid memories of going to the Winn Dixie at a very young age, maybe four or five and collecting coupons or ads hanging at my eye level. I don't know why I did that. My best guess is that I wanted to try and read them by making up the text.

To this day, I still want to hang on to anything paper. Whether its doctor reports, handwritten recipes, sentimental notes, magazine articles, random recipes clipped from magazines, ticket stubs, old receipts, business cards, flyers from events, letters, cards, or appliance manuals. They all find their way into my file boxes. Lucky for me I don't have many kitchen gadgets, so that cuts down on the manuals. Besides most appliances don't come with paper manuals anymore. That's a good thing. If you want a manual, you usually have to download it from your computer. I hang on to the paper stuff maybe because it is sentimental. Or perhaps I think I might need it someday down the road.

Now the thing is, I had this paper stuff neatly tucked into file boxes. And those boxes were labeled. But I wasn't happy.

I had a box labeled "Current." Another box labeled "Home." And a third box labeled "Projects," a fourth box labeled "Book stuff," and a fifth box labeled "Miscellaneous." I had too many boxes. And I wasn't stopping at just five. Oh, no, there were more and more. Not until I decided to consolidate all those boxes into three boxes was I at peace. I forced myself to go through each box and toss what I didn't need and keep what I needed.

So that was progress.

Un-necessary paper is cumbersome. I feel so much lighter when the paper situation is under control. Not just lighter in my boxes, but lighter in my head. I'm not worrying about it all the time. And when I need a particular paper, I can retrieve it rather quickly. Beyond the three boxes of paper stuff, I keep one spiral notebook of lists.

I used to create many, many notebooks. I had a notebook for things to do, one for things I needed to buy, one for information, and one for "later." And some others. I decided to consolidate all those notebooks into one spiral notebook. Here's how it works. I take a new page of the notebook and divide it into four square boxes which I label as 1. To do. 2. To buy. 3. Information 4. Later. Every day I read through the list and make a star by what I want to accomplish for that day. Once I complete that item, I scratch it off. When I run out of room on one page, I move to the next. It's that simple.

Taming the paper situation is not un-like taming other areas of your life. It's the same three tub mentality. And if you are tech-savvy you can scan many of the documents onto a thumb drive, label it and you've saved a whole lot of room.

Keep what physical papers are only necessary or essential to you, and toss the rest — nothing less, nothing more.

CHAPTER EIGHTEEN

Life Lessons

As we go through life, we all learn lessons. Even if we don't acknowledge the fact, we are all life-long learners. What a fantastic gift we possess.

Our successes and setbacks are teaching moments. But we don't always heed them.

Case in point: I have been on diets hundreds of times. I have learned what foods are healthy to eat, and which to avoid. I know all about how bad sugar is for you. I know what a carb is and a protein. I even know which is better for me. I know how to count calories, points, and glasses of water. I know how many fewer calories I need to eat to lose weight. I have measuring spoons to use when I choose. The keyword here is "choose."

It has been said, "knowledge is power." I think that is true, but only to the extent that you use that knowledge.

I can be a guru on diets, but if I don't choose to put my knowledge into practice, I'm not going to lose weight. It's that simple. And I fear that I am not alone.

I was in a major grocery store over the weekend, and while shopping, I perused the coupon/brochure rack. A flyer caught my eye. The title was: "Now it's easier to make better choices." Very intriguing, I thought, as I picked one up.

The gist of the flyer was that some manufacturers were now changing their food labels to include much more product information. They were now showing specific nutrients in the product as well as serving size and calories. The whole point is to help consumers make wise choices.

Great news if we choose to use that information. But sometimes we opt for the method of "it looks good, tastes good, I'll take it." I must admit I am guilty of that method myself sometimes, especially if I am in a hurry.

When you think of minimalism, it's just like any other skill you've learned. There are tools of the trade, not just the ones I've come up with, but many other people have shared their ideas as well. Whether or not anyone uses these tools will be a choice they make.

In my teaching days, I learned about the word "automaticity" when teaching reading. According to Wikipedia, "automaticity" is the ability to do things without occupying the mind with the low-level details required allowing it to become an automatic response." The goal of teaching reading to my struggling readers was to help them learn to read smoothly and automatically.

Automaticity can be useful to the minimalist as well. If you practice what you learn about living with less, it will become automatic. And things that become automatic are often more fun and ultimately produce more significant success.

I've talked with you about my goals, the "four" boxes, strategies for managing this thing called minimalism and more. And if you just read this book and use none of my suggestions or the suggestions of others, that is fine. But if you choose to move forward with minimalism, remember practice usually produces results. Just like trying to change my eating habits isn't hard, but it takes practice.

Taking baby steps is the perfect way for many of us to proceed. That's the way I have approached this lifestyle.

For others, however, who want to leap right in and grab the "gusto" of doing it all in record time, that is your choice.

Again, it's all about choice.

Like everyone else who has ever learned to ride a bike, I haven't forgotten. Twenty years ago, my husband bought me a new coaster bike. Very much like the one I had as a child. Other than stationary bikes once in a while, I hadn't been riding a bicycle. I was very excited about my first ride.

I remember as a child riding all over the neighborhood. I loved every minute! The wind in my air, singing songs as I rode past familiar places. It was exhilarating. I anticipated the same feeling this time.

Unfortunately, the first experience on my new bike was a little different than I had conjured up in my mind. You see, when I was about seven years old, I learned how to ride a bike. And once I learned, I rode and rode till I couldn't ride one more block. But at some point, maybe age eleven or twelve, I quit riding every day.

So, when I got my new bike twenty years ago, I was dumbfounded. Yes, I still remembered how to ride a bike, but it was not the carefree, comfortable ride it once was. I ran out of energy way, way too soon. I wondered then and there what had happened? I used to love to ride a bike. Now it was like work. It wasn't fun. My bones ached, and my peddling became laborious much too soon. Granted, I was much older and had that thing they call arthritis, but still. I should be able to ride a bike like I always had.

The difference was I didn't keep up riding. Yes, I did the stationary bike a few times, but very few. I still knew how to ride a bike, but I hadn't practice what I had learned. I was rusty and a bit, "crusty." If I would start back and ride a little each day, I know, I could get stronger and gradually work up to some semblance of yesteryear, even with that nagging arthritis.

The bike story is a reminder to me of the adage, "use it or lose it." To maintain a skill, you must use that skill, whether it be a sport and something like minimalism.

I like to think of minimalism as something fun

I have learned to do and want to keep it up for a long time. It's a way of life that I am embracing and enjoying every minute. The more I read about minimalism, and the more I practice minimalism, the more enthusiastic I become. Minimalism is solace at its best.

CHAPTER NINETEN

The Top Four Things That Make Me Happy

As promised at the beginning of this book, I am sharing with you a list of things that make me happy. Along with downsizing, part of being a minimalist is maintaining a positive attitude and keeping an optimistic outlook.

Here are the four things that make me happy:

Number one: Family. Family is everything. Starting with the best husband in the world. And I have a huge extended family. I wish everyone could have the most fabulous loving family that I have.

Number two: Friends. Every article on living

longer will usually mention the importance of having friends. I have new friends and friends I have known all my life. Each brings something unique to my life, and I surely hope I add to their life in some small way.

Number three: Photos. Since Junior High, I have enjoyed taking photos. To me, photos mark time in a way nothing else can.

Number four: Poetry. This particular word needs some explanation. First of all, when most people think of poetry, they think of a literary work, something that is written down. And I do love reading and writing poetry — all kinds. But poetry is more than that. The definition of poetry goes beyond literary works. The third definition of poetry in the dictionary says: "Poetry" is something regarded as comparable to poetry, in its beauty."

In 2003, as a teacher, I was required to take a workshop given by Georgia Heard. It was very memorable and worthwhile.

Georgia Heard is a writer, poet, and educator. She is a frequent presenter in schools and conferences around the world.

One of the exercises she asked of us was to write down the answer to the question, "Where does poetry hide?"

I thought it was a great exercise, not only because I love poetry, but because poetry goes beyond the poem written on the page. I wrote my thoughts on a small piece of paper, which I saved because it was a meaningful exercise, and I thought I would refer to it someday. And today is that day.

Here is what I wrote:

"Poetry hides in a mailbox full of junk mail."

"Poetry hides behind the walls if they could only talk."

"Poetry hides in the silent voice of a want to be poet."

"Poetry hides behind smiling eyes that really want to cry."

The point of the exercise was to get our brains moving, but beyond that, I think it showed that poetry could be anywhere.

A further example: My mom, dad, and I were once driving down a tree-lined street in Williamsburg, Virginia, when my mom remarked, "There is nothing prettier than a tree." For her, she saw poetry in a tree. And now I see it too.

Those are just four things that make me happy and believe me there are more. What makes you happy?

CHAPTER TWENTY

Don't Make It Complicated If
You Want to Keep It Simple

Musicals are among my favorite movies. Camelot is in the top five. At one point in the film, Guinevere asks Arthur, what do the simple folk do? Which then segues into the song of the same title. The song lists several things that simple folk do such as singing, dancing, and whistling. And Guinevere and Arthur do them all. They are joyful and happy at that moment.

In another one of my favorite musicals, "The

Sound of Music," there is a song called "My Favorite Things." Julie Andrews, who plays the part of the nanny "Maria," sings that song to the children when a thunderstorm is approaching. The words and the music soothe them. One of the favorite things they sing about is "raindrops on roses." An easy thing to visualize. This idea of singing about one's favorite things is something I am sure psychiatrists would applaud.

There is a parallel with these examples and the practice of minimalism. In both, it's the simple things that make everyone happy. Life doesn't have to be complicated, especially if we want to keep it simple.

So, in keeping with that theme, I made my own "simple thing" list as follows:

One: Listening to Roger play the guitar or harmonica.
Two: Reminiscing with family and friends.
Three: Observing Christmas lights in December.
Four: Growing periwinkles on my front porch.
Five: Watching a sunrise or a sunset.
Six: Walking on the beach.

These are six simple things I like to do. Just re-reading them makes me feel a sense of calm. Try making a list for yourself. And don't feel you can't change your list after you make it. It's a therapeutic exercise. You can do it over and over again, and it doesn't get old.

When I think about minimalism, I think of a whole way of life. Minimalism is not just cleaning out a closet or downsizing. It is about living simply. It is about doing things that are fun and meaningful. Purposeful. It is enjoying the moment and being thankful for family and friends. It is spending time with them.

As I was contemplating ideas for this chapter on "keeping it simple," it took me back again to the early sixties when I was in Junior High School. Our youth group at Childs Park Church had gathered together for one of our parties. We were going on a scavenger hunt which was popular at that time. We were divided into teams. The idea was to walk around the neighborhood, going door to door, trying to be the first team to find everything on the list. Things like bobby pins, rubber bands and bubble gum usually showed up on the list. But I will never forget when one of the items to find was a piece of toast. And believe it or not, someone gave us one! Once again, this was a simple, fun activity. Probably not the best idea today to go door to door, but remember the sixties were a different time.

I am sure you know people who get carried away planning parties for birthdays or wedding showers or baby showers, especially in the twenty-first century.

As an example, most weddings have become extravaganzas. Many people spend thousands of dollars, only to be in the poor house after a couple of hours feeding hundreds of people a gourmet meal. That is a personal choice, but it is a far cry from minimalism.

If you are planning a family party or reunion try not to go over-board. A trip to the dollar store for some plastic table cloths and a couple balloons, along with a few well-chosen decorations will go a long way. Add in some grocery store sandwich platters, chips, cookies and tea, and you have will pretty much all you need. Keep in mind that the goal is to gather with family and enjoy each other's company.

And remember not to make it complicated if you want to keep it simple.

CHAPTER TWENTY-ONE

Regrets?

There is a song titled: "My Way," written by Paul Anka and popularized by Frank Sinatra in 1969. The first lines go something like this, "Regrets, I've had a few, but then again too few to mention. I did what I had to do and saw it through without exemption."

I often think about that song when people ask me if I have given away anything and then regretted that action.

The simple and quickest answer is "yes." Yes, there are things that I wished I hadn't given away.

But the longer answer is even though I have a few regrets, just like in the song, there are too few to mention. But, in full disclosure, I do want to share with you that sometimes you might part with an item that later on you decided that you needed or wanted.

It all goes back to the question of your core philosophy. If you genuinely want to become a minimalist, then even though, as I have stated before, everyone's result is different, you will try to pare down in some fashion. And, at some point, you will most likely wish you hadn't given or thrown something away. But that's okay. It takes time to learn what to keep, what to give away, and what to toss in the garbage.

Sometimes I will find something at a garage sale only to get home and realize it won't fit in our house. I can't take it back, so I immediately put it in the garage to donate to charity. I don't keep it to justify my purchase.

I realize my mistake and deal with it right then and there. That is the most efficient way.

CHAPTER TWENTY-TWO

Wrapping It Up

In this last chapter, I would like to tie up any loose ends and summarize my point of view of minimalism. I hope you are taking away something new about the movement and that you enjoyed reliving this journey with me.

As I wrote the above first line, I quickly realized that this isn't the "last chapter." There will be no "last chapter," because, with minimalism, every day is a new beginning. And, though I am finishing with this book, my minimalist journey continues. I hope to keep gaining insight on this topic and continue to be as enthusiastic tomorrow as I am today.

My minimalist journey began in high school long before I even knew about the movement and brought me to this point in my life. With each day, I inch a little closer to being able to say that I am a true minimalist. Here is the funny thing about that. The only person who can confirm or deny the fact that I have reached "minimalism" status is me. The folks at Guinness Book of World records will not be coming to my house to take inventory and declare me a bona fide minimalist.

There isn't a mid-term or final exam. There isn't even a weekly quiz. The only way to measure success is from with-in. There is no minimalist organization that will give me a gold star with a "job well done." It's all in my hands.

I am the only judge of how much progress I have made. I can set my goals, and at some point, do a self-evaluation to see if I have accomplished those goals.

People may visit my home and not have a clue I am an aspiring minimalist. They may comment that my home looks "neat," or ask if I've gotten rid of things.

I've had people say to me when visiting,

"Everywhere I look there is something I like" or "I can tell everything in your home is picked out with purpose." I don't tell them it's because I got rid of the proverbial "forest," so now they can see the "trees," I smile and say thank you.

As I stated at the beginning of this book, there is no one way to approach minimalism. Conversely, that means there are many ways to approach it and just as many ways to determine growth.

It's all about being reflective.

I had an "ah-ha" moment recently that I would love to share. It illustrates how I can tell that I am walking toward my goal and not straying from it.

About a year and a half ago, in October of 2017, I began a new part-time job working for a company in China, called VIPKID. The job was teaching English to Chinese children. It was an on-line job, working one on one with students ages four to twelve. To do this, you needed a four-year degree, which I had.

At first, I was very enthusiastic. I followed the step-by-step process to get hired. I had to do an interview and teach a fifteen-minute lesson with a representative in China. I also had to do a mock lesson for a teacher in the U.S. (posing as a student). And finally, a myriad of paperwork.

Honestly, one of the reasons I tried out for the job was to see if a retired teacher could get hired. And, yes, I did get hired.

My artistic husband volunteered to be my "prop" man for VIP Kid. He was willing to make any puppets or charts that I needed, which is exactly what he did when I taught in a brick and mortar school.

MY VIP CLASSROOM

Because of Roger's artistic talents, I had a very child-centered classroom back in the day. Both when I taught kindergarten and first grade. He made me a five-foot wooden shoe and painted it to represent the "Old Woman in the Shoe" poem. The shoe was complete with an old woman puppet, peeking out the window. There were bookshelves painted with children, dry erase boards for the kids, and even a six-foot paper mâché' giraffe. The kids loved those "props" and many more.

Teaching VIP Kid on-line was similar to teaching in a brick and mortar classroom. However, it required even many more visuals because you have to use what the "English As A Second Language" classes refer to as "realia." That means pictures, stuffed animals, plastic or paper items that represent real things as well as the "real" things.

Roger and I decided to turn his art room into somewhat of a "studio" for teaching my lessons. We re-arranged the room to look like a mini classroom. We had to find a place for the small table and lights to make sure I was seen well on the computer. We made a backdrop of pictures and hung a map of the world, with a line of lights, going from Florida to China.

Without spending too much money, I purchased a few things at garage sales and the dollar store, to get started. We bought new lights to attach to our hat tree for lighting. The lighting was essential for on-line lessons.

I purchased some poster board and markers for making "props." My friend Denise loaned me some magnetic letters, picture cards, and puppets. All in all, we didn't spend much money, but we had multiple things for my virtual classroom.

Together my husband and I turned the art room into a classroom with plenty of visuals. Outside the room in one of the hall closets, I housed my extra pictures, flashcards, books, and other toys to use in my lessons.

Roger and I spent time putting everything in motion.

The week after being hired, I had my first student booked for a class. At first, it was fun and exciting. I was getting several bookings. But shortly after, the bookings were less and less because I wasn't willing to work through the night, the prime time for Chinese students on-line, due to the time difference between here and there.

By December of 2017, I had decided that when my six-month contract was up in March, I wasn't going to sign a new contract. It was a great experience, but the time difference wasn't working out for me. And I wasn't finding the time I wanted to work on my writing.

Now here is where the minimalism comes in.

When March came, and my contract was up, I had some decisions to make. What was I going to do with ALL the "stuff" that I had accumulated for my on-line teaching? Though much of it I bought at the dollar store and garage sales, and it didn't cost that much, I did not need it.

So, here is what I did. First, I gave back the

stuff I had borrowed from Denise along with some things I thought she could use in her classroom.

I then gave the rest of the pictures and "realia" to the thrift store.

That left me with two notebooks of things that I printed to help me teach the curriculum. Most of that I tossed. But the old "saver" in me was trying to rear its ugly head.

As I held the paper that I printed when I got hired that was titled: "Congratulations," I knew the old me would file it away for a rainy day. But I had to ask myself, "Why do I need to keep this? Is it something that I want? I quickly answered my questions with "no" and tossed that paper into the garbage. It felt good.

But, then, as I thought I had gotten rid of everything, I saw out of the corner of my eye, on the table, a stack of index cards wrapped with a big rubber band. On each card was the name of a student that I had taught. My first instinct was to keep those cards. After all, I reasoned, I had taught each child on those cards. How could I throw those cards in the trash? Didn't I need those cards to remember VIPKID? But then, the minimalist in me prevailed. I knew what I wanted to do.

I tossed them into the garbage and if felt very

good. The old me would have put those cards in a box, in the closet, and saved them. For no good reason, only to find them years later. And even though it was only a three or four-inch stack of cards, it was something taking up space that didn't serve a purpose.

I'm not there yet, but today I'm feeling good about how far I've come with my journey toward becoming a minimalist. I'm feeling free from the burden of so many material things. And free from the angst of letting go of those things. I'm enjoying the extra space in my closet and my mind. I'm even more proud of the sign my husband painted for me. The one that reads, "Cum Exprimere minus," my new motto, "Express with Less."

Writing this book has helped me stick with my convictions and pare down even more. My next house move might not be with just the clothes on my back, as I joked at the beginning of this book, but I promise you the load will be a whole lot lighter.

EPILOGUE

Before I go, I want to leave you with one last thought. There are readers out there who I know will challenge my less is more philosophy, thinking there are things we need more of and not less. I was racking my brain trying to determine if there is one material thing that I wouldn't want to run out of and maybe more of it might be better than less.

Two things that came to mind were gasoline for my car and toilet paper. I never want to run out of those items. There you go.

Remember, there is no one right way to practice minimalism or wrong way. And no trophies given for a job well done. Just pat yourself on the back and tell yourself "bravo" once in a while.

Thank you for reading my book. Hopefully, you are walking away with some emotion. Good or not so good. I would love to hear your thoughts either way. You can share them with me on our Hoffman Bookends page on Facebook or friend me on Facebook by typing in Nancy Cunningham Hoffman.

If I were asked to sum up in one sentence what minimalism is to me, it would be this: The minimalist owns one coat that she finds warm, comfortable and beautiful while the non-minimalist has several coats in her closet, none of which fit that criteria.

I hope some of what I have written has resonated with you and you can walk away with more of what you love and less of what you don't.

Printed in the United States
By Bookmasters